unstoppable confidence

Unleash Your Natural Confidence Within

KENT SAYRE

Unstoppable Books
Portland, OR

Unstoppable Confidence
by Kent Sayre
Published by Unstoppable Books, www.unstoppable-books.com
Copyright ©2001 by Unstoppable Books
4888 N.W. Bethany Blvd.
Suite K-5, #214
Portland, OR 97229

Cover and text design © TLC Graphics, www.TLCGraphics.com

Front cover and title page photo © Digital Vision

Manufactured in the United States of America.

Special edition printed specifically for the Direct Selling Industry by DreamHouse
Publishing, P.O. Box 2650, Broken Arrow, OK 74013

Publisher's Cataloging-in-Publication
    (Prepared by Quality Books, Inc.)

Sayre, Kent.

    Unstoppable confidence : unleash your natural
confidence within / by Kent Sayre ; edited by Elroy
Carter. – 1st ed.
        p. cm.

    1. Self-confidence.   I. Carter, Elroy.   II. Title.
BF575.S39S29 2001   158.1
                            QBI01-201253

Library of Congress Number: 2001096324
ISBN: 0-9715003-0-4

This book is dedicated to all those people
in the world living their dreams,
who have unstoppable confidence.

Most of all, this book is dedicated to my parents,
Steve and Betsy Sayre, who believed in me
long before I believed in myself.
Thank you.

acknowledgements

I want to extend a warm thank you to everyone who made this project possible.

Thank you, Troy Montserrat-Gonzales, for your work in helping me to get my ideas on paper.

Thank you to Elroy Carter for editing this book for me. Thank you for your endless devotion to this project. It has been a *great* opportunity to work with you.

Thank you to Fred Gleeck for leading my marketing team. Thanks to Tami Dever, Erin Stark, and Jill Andersen for taking my raw manuscript and turning it into a professional book.

Thank you to my parents, Steve and Betsy Sayre, and my brother, Ryan Sayre, for your encouragement and support of this project.

Thank you to all of my mentors who have taught me so well: Kenrick Cleveland, Rex Steven Sikes, Richard Bandler, John Grinder, Brian Tracy, and Anthony Robbins. I am grateful every day for the impact you have had on my life.

table
of contents

Table of Contents

unstoppable confidence

My name is Kent Sayre and this book is a product of my transformation from being an extremely shy person to being one with a lot of confidence. I know that if I can do it, anyone can break out of being shy and become more confident. I was literally the shyest person that I had ever known. Even if you already have a lot of confidence now, you will benefit from this book by stretching your confidence beyond what you thought was even possible.

My purpose for writing this book is to invite everyone who reads this to take a shortcut and immediately become more confident by doing the exercises and adopting the confidence mindset that is described throughout the book. When I was extremely shy and needed confidence, I had to take the long road to confidence. Through my own trial and error, I've found what works, what doesn't work, and what really works.

Much of the material, yet not all, is based upon Neuro-Linguistic Programming (NLP).

NLP is the study of how language, both verbal and nonverbal, affects our minds. By consciously directing our minds, we can create resourceful ways of behaving for ourselves. In this book, all of the methods are geared toward having more confidence in our lives and stepping beyond our previously defined limits.

One of the NLP presuppositions is that we all share the same neurology, which means whatever anyone can do, you can do as well, provided that you direct your mind in exactly the same way. That means if something is possible for others, it's possible for you, too. If confidence is possible for others (and it definitely is), it is definitely possible for you, too. Using NLP methods, I have modeled very confident people and included what they do in this book. By doing what they do, you will achieve the same resourceful states of confidence that they have. From how confident people think about things to how they speak to how they carry their bodies, you will find in this book how confident people move through the world.

Chapter One describes my background of being painfully shy and how I overcame my shyness. It continues on with having the reader set some very specific goals about what they want out of this book so that they can focus in and accomplish what they want. True confidence is defined and it's explained why confidence is such an integral part of life.

Chapter Two teaches the reader to speak the language of confidence. They learn how to speak authoritatively and harness the power of confident words. Furthermore, the reader learns how to eliminate the confidence-destroying words from his or her vocabulary.

Chapter Three details the nine factors of unstoppable confidence. There are different factors that go into making someone confident and they are described in this chapter. The reader will learn how to use momentum to their benefit, how to commit to success, and how to discover their own natural motivation strategy.

Chapter Four goes in-depth about the topic of beliefs. Beliefs shape our lives. The value of empowering beliefs cannot be overstated. This chapter invites the reader to eliminate disempowering beliefs and replace those beliefs with useful beliefs, and teaches a specific method for how to do exactly that.

Chapter Five covers the body language of confidence. This chapter describes how confident people move, walk, and gesture. By learning how they do it, and doing it yourself, you will convey confidence to yourself and others.

Chapter Six teaches you how to master your internal voice. You will not only squash the negative, nagging internal voice, you will replace that old voice with a new empowering voice that encourages you to go after your dreams. Specific and easy-to-do methods are given to eliminate the negative voice and amplify the positive voice.

Chapter Seven teaches how to create instant rapport with anyone you meet. When you know you can easily create rapport with anyone who you speak with, your confidence levels will soar.

Chapter Eight gives 20 specific exercises geared toward expanding your confidence to unprecedented levels. Doing these exercises is what helped me expand my confidence the most and I still use these exercises very frequently to become even more confident.

Chapter Nine points you to your confident future and your new life with unstoppable confidence. It offers advice for how to make confidence your lifelong habit and how to integrate confidence into your daily life and make it is part of who you are, not simply something you do.

getting started on your journey

All our dreams can come true,
if we have the courage to pursue them.

— Walt Disney

A Story Of Confidence And Shyness

Samantha and Cathy both graduated from college fifteen years ago. Samantha became a lawyer and Cathy worked as an engineer in the high-technology field. They each have successful careers, fulfilling marriages, and are proud parents. They own their own homes and lead a happy life except for the fulfillment in their careers.

While they are both successful at their careers, they are both disenchanted with them. Samantha does not find what she is doing fulfilling and neither does Cathy. They used to eagerly look forward to work every day and the challenge of their respective careers. Fifteen years later, however, after doing the same thing, they have changed and no longer find their careers rewarding. They both want to pursue their true passions.

Samantha has always loved baking and wants to open her own bakery. She learned how to bake as a child and has always enjoyed it. Samantha knew that if she could own a bakery, it would be a smashing success, as she envisioned people coming from miles around to purchase her baked goods.

Cathy has always cherished music. She grew up listening to music each spare moment she could and singing in her church choir. She currently sings in her woman's group, yet she visualizes what it would be like for her to be a professional with her own CD released, touring the region and giving concerts.

Fast forward five years. Samantha, while still yearning to open her bakery, has taken no action to actually make her dream come true. Each day that

passes she feels like she is wasting her time at her job while she lives someone else's dream. Instead of jumping out of the bed in the morning, she has
to nag herself internally until she rolls out of bed and heads into work. She
yearns for Fridays and absolutely despises Mondays. Spending the majority
of her waking hours doing something she finds despicable, she feels as if she
is wasting her life.

Cathy has taken tremendous action in the past five years and consequently has her own CD out, tours the region, and gives sell-out concerts for her
music. The ideal lifestyle that she dreamt of five years ago has manifested
itself due to her efforts. She cherishes each and every moment of her life.
The time she spends on stage singing is the time when she feels that she is
the most alive. She doesn't just exist; she knows she is living well. It seems
as if her life gets better and better each and every day. Sure, she has had her
struggles in launching her own CD and getting her name to be recognized.
She had countless people tell her no. In the face of defeat, she persisted.
She never quit. It would have been easier to stay at her old job and yet it
would have been tremendously unfulfilling as well. Cathy paid the price
through her commitment to live her dreams, and she ultimately made them
come true.

Samantha and Cathy both had dreams and visions for their respective
futures. One of them made it happen and one didn't. It reminds me of the
riddle of two frogs. Two frogs are sitting on a lily in a lake and one decides to
jump off. How many frogs jump off? There are still two frogs remaining on the
lily because deciding to do something and doing something are two entirely different things. Cathy took action and fulfilled her dreams. Samantha did
not. The difference between the two is that Cathy had the confidence to put
her plan into motion by taking action. Samantha lacked the confidence.
What you will find are the techniques, attitudes, and beliefs Cathy and other
successful people have while they pursue their dreams. They may not be
aware of these techniques specifically, yet they believe in them in order to get
their results.

What Is Confidence?

Since this book is all about *confidence*, we will define the term right off the
bat so we are all on the same page and know what we are talking about
here. Confidence means different things to different people. Similarly, confidence evokes certain feelings and automatic reactions within people.
Before we go any further, we will discover what confidence is not and then
show what it is.

What Confidence Is Not

Arrogance vs. Confidence

Arrogance is sometimes mistaken for confidence. Arrogance is something completely different from confidence. Arrogance is the notion of being somewhat confident with a leaning toward elitism, bragging, being macho, showing off, etc.

Have you ever seen those really huge guys with bulging muscles, overdeveloped to the point where they thrust their chests way out and swagger in the utmost cocky way? This is an example of arrogance and not true confidence. It is almost as if they consider themselves better than others since they are so large. True confidence comes from within, and when you realize you are ✓ confident, you do not need to proclaim it to the world.

Now contrast the example of arrogance with the following example of true confidence. Stop for a moment and consider the famous, muscular movie stars Arnold Schwarzenegger and Sylvester Stallone. These guys do not go around with puffed up chests and think they are better than everyone else. Instead, they have a calm, quiet, powerful confidence that comes from an awareness of their abilities. This is a major difference and we'll explore this further later in the book.

True Confidence Does Not Need To Be Stated

I have met many people who are confident and many people who lacked confidence. The truly confident people all had a similar trait among them: ✓ their confidence came from within and it did not have to be voiced. A nonchalant, matter-of-fact confidence is ideal. There is no need to brag about one's accomplishments. Those who brag are only masking their insecurity about themselves. Allow your results to speak for themselves. Actions speak ✓✓ louder than words, so take your confidence and make it happen.

If someone has to continually broadcast his or her "confidence," it really makes me wonder. It seems that they are not really that confident at all and instead they are often trying to convince themselves by telling others. They are trying to gain confidence in an ineffective manner. Confidence comes from within and when you believe in yourself, others will believe in you. This is a universal law. It does not work the other way around, no matter how much we would prefer that. Later on in this book, you will learn far easier and more effective ways to skyrocket your confidence.

True Confidence Comes From Within

Take a moment and think of an area of your life where you may or may not be confident. Ask yourself this question: "How do you know that you are proficient at <name your area>?" And being completely honest with yourself, notice your answer. If you absolutely know that you are proficient in the area you chose because it was your own thought or feeling or belief system, congratulations! You are really confident in that area. If you were not sure about your proficiency in your area or if you had to rely on an external confirmation from your peers, spouse, supervisor, etc., you are not quite as confident as you can be. By the end of the book, after doing the exercises, you will be right there. When you have done all the exercises and completed this book, you will have the true confidence that comes from within.

Confidence or the lack thereof can and does occur across all demographics. Across all races, all economic levels, and all religions, there are some people who are confident and some who are not. Even the rich and famous movie star, who many envy and consider to have it all, gets nervous at times because they want to perform well.

Belligerence vs. Confidence

Let's talk about the difference between belligerence and confidence, using relationships as an example. Sometimes, women are apparently attracted to 'jerks.' I'm sure that many of us have seen examples of this in our lives, or know someone in this situation. On the surface the jerk exhibits some 'bad boy' traits that some women may perceive as confidence. The jerk himself has probably convinced himself that he has it all 'going on.' What masquerades as confidence in the jerk is just belligerence and a super-aggressive attitude. You can and should always assert yourself whenever you deem it necessary. However, this does not mean bullying people and trampling over them. The jerk in this example does not realize this.

Belligerence is what makes a jerk just that. The jerk is abrasive and cares little for the relationships he forms with others, but bulldozes his way through life. *True* confidence, however, allows you to go through life easily, to efficiently get the results you want, and make people feel good when you deal with them. Make people *feel good*. Do this because *you can*.

Why Confidence Is Important

Let's get down to why confidence is important. Confidence is *vital* because it is the difference that makes the difference. When people consistently take action and make the appropriate course corrections, they get massive results and achieve all their goals. However, if they lack that same confidence, they will stay stuck. It would be no different if they had no dreams or goals at all. After all, what's the point if they don't pursue them?

Having the confidence, especially in the context of having the ability to communicate, is absolutely essential. Without it, people don't communicate effectively. To the degree that you are confident and communicate well with others is the degree to which you will succeed in life. No matter what context you're referring to: business, family, friends, career. It is directly proportional to the degree you will experience a rewarding and fulfilling life.

Competence vs. Confidence

Are confidence and competence the same thing? No! In fact, they are quite distinct. Understanding the difference is essential.

Competence: *The ability to do something.* ✓

Confidence: *Your belief about your competence.* ✓

Each of us has individual experiences, beliefs, and values that make us perceive life in our own individual way. Everyone has their own perception of ✓ reality, a unique model of the world. This means that it is only a *perception* ✓ and not actual reality. The empowering part of this idea is that these beliefs ✓ can be changed and thereby change one's perception of life. This means that the exercises and strategies described in this book will change your beliefs and your perception of what is possible for yourself.

Confidence Without Competence

People are an absolute recipe for disaster if they lack competence and yet have unjustified confidence. Take for example someone who has never flown a plane before but has ridden on a plane and thinks they are now ace pilots since they read a book once on it a decade ago. Would you let that person fly you across the country? I would get off that plane so fast that people would think I was a blur. You can easily see how there are numerous examples of confidence without competence and why it's dangerous.

Competence Without Confidence

If someone is competent and yet lacks confidence, they will be stuck. They might have a perfect understanding of some powerful concepts yet they never take action. Someone who has the knowledge and competence to do something and does nothing is no better off than someone who is clueless and incompetent. The proper fruit of knowledge is action. ✓

When I was getting started in real estate investment, I was the classic example of competence without confidence. I studied, studied, and studied real estate. I read ten books, took three home-study courses, attended a seminar, and signed up for two mentoring programs. Still, I was stuck big time. I saw others being successful and knew exactly what they were doing and how they were doing it. I asked them and they confirmed to me that they were doing exactly what I was only thinking about. What was holding me back? It was my lack of confidence and fear of the unknown.

If you asked me then, you had to know absolutely everything about all of real estate before you took any action and did anything! So I kept studying and studying, trying in vain to learn everything so I could actually get started. Meanwhile, everyone else around me had their businesses taking off because they were taking action.

* There are three key beliefs that will enable you to escape being stuck, and allow you to easily take action:

∨ 1. You do not need to know everything to get started.

∨ 2. You are a very resourceful person.

∨ 3. If you do not know the answer to something, you can
        find the answer or the person who does know.

Think about how relieving and empowering this is. You are free to know your piece of the puzzle while you let everyone else fill in their roles to accomplish what you want.

It was ludicrous for me to need to know everything about real estate investment before doing anything. Now as I think back on it, it is analogous to me having to understand how a spontaneous combustion engine works before I can even drive my car. Since you realize the difference between a stuck attitude and an empowering attitude, you will naturally become aware of any times that you might be acting stuck. At that point, back up and change your attitude by remembering your resourcefulness.

Competence + Confidence = Success

Being unstoppable means having the competence and the confidence and going for it. This is what this book is all about:

* When you have the competence to do what you want and the confidence to follow through and take action, you are *unstoppable*!

This is the pinnacle of success. Nothing can or will stop you from achieving what you want. You realize that anything in your path that seems like an obstacle or a detour really is an opportunity in disguise to show your resourcefulness.

It is like an airplane pilot flying from L.A. to New York. The pilot does not chart a course and then turn on autopilot and go to sleep at the wheel. That is because the plane is constantly being blown off course by the weather, having route changes to avoid nearby planes, and avoiding turbulence. The pilot is always watching the readings that indicate the plane's location and status. From this feedback, the pilot constantly adjusts the plane to allow all the passengers to safely arrive in New York. Up to ninety-five percent of the time, the plane is flying "off course." However, they always get to the destination. As you think about this, you can find how this relates to your own goals.

Here's the simple success formula in a nutshell:

1. You set an outcome.

2. You monitor your results you get through feedback.

3. You vary your behavior until you get your outcome.

Knowing your outcome means having a vision of what you do want for your-self in your life. When you know what you want, you can get it much more easily. It's impossible to get what you want if you haven't first decided what you do in fact want.

Monitoring your results through feedback means having the sensory acuity to know what is working for you and what is not working for you. When you find something that works for you, you naturally do more of it and in an even better way if you can. When you find something that is not working, you ask yourself what you can do differently to get your results.

What it means to vary your behavior until you get your outcome is that you persist and keep doing different things, operating with different strategies, and using different techniques until you finally achieve your outcome.

As you follow this formula, you'll realize yourself meeting and exceeding all of your expectations. Following this formula means that you will achieve your outcome. After you get your outcomes, the next thing you'll naturally do is to set even grander outcomes that cause you to stretch and grow as a person.

Getting The Most Out Of This Book By Setting Some Goals

A Harvard study on goal setting took place in the 1950s with a follow-up study in the 1980s. The study in the 1950s showed that only three percent of the respondents had set goals at the time of their graduation, and yet in the 1980s, this three percent was financially worth more than the remaining ninety-seven percent combined. These people had focus and direction, and this was displayed by the setting of their goals. To gain the maximum bene-fit from this book, we will begin by setting *your* goals for this journey we are taking together.

Stop for a moment and answer these questions:

· What do you want to get out of this book?

· What's stopping you from getting this right now?

- What's important to you about achieving your goals?
- What will it be like for you to have unstoppable confidence?
- What will having unstoppable confidence do for you?
- Are you ready to eliminate all your fear, uncertainty, hesitation, and doubt forever?
- How will you know when you've got unstoppable confidence?

We will now set a SMART outcome for you. An *outcome* is something you desire. It is similar to a goal yet can be much smaller. The terms will be used interchangeably. The acronym SMART stands for: Specific, Measurable, Achievable, Realistic, and Timed.

Specific

You make an outcome *specific* when you state what you will see, hear, feel and experience, things which will verify that you have undoubtedly achieved it. A general outcome would be, "I want to get confidence out of this book." That does not work as well as the following, specific outcome: "I want to gain two specific strategies for eliminating my fear of changing jobs and gain confidence in knowing I will succeed at whatever job I have." In the same way, make your outcomes specific.

Measurable

Your outcome is *measurable* when you have a clear way to know if you have met your outcome or not. An immeasurable outcome is, "I will be confident by the end of the book by using the techniques described in this book." While confidence is sometimes difficult to measure, you can get creative and find ways. A more measurable outcome is, "I will make more direct eye contact with people in my new job, I will maintain confident physiology, posture, and bearing, and I will be more outgoing by initiating conversations with my co-workers."

Achievable

Ensure that your outcome is *achievable*, that it is physically viable for you to accomplish. Ensure that you have a good likelihood of success. Remember that while **you are unstoppable** and that you can achieve *anything* that you desire, you must simultaneously plan a smooth progression, a driving movement from point A to point B that stretches your comfort zone as you march toward success.

Avoid setting yourself up for frustration by setting an outcome that is unattainable in the short term. Plan your progression; know the small steps along the way that will lead you to your ultimate goals. Set achievable goals, achieve them, and reset your goals even higher!

If you feel like the shyest person in the world right now, setting a goal to instantly be the life of the party only sets yourself up for a rude awakening. You can and will be the life of the party if you want, eventually, but first begin with the first steps, like talking to strangers and confidently asking about how they are doing.

Realistic ✓

Realistic outcomes are outcomes that are based in *reality*. If you want to grow wings and fly, that is not going to happen. Asking for an unrealistic outcome only sets you up for failure. When you set realistic outcomes, you will be proud of yourself when you achieve them. Realistic means that it is something that can be done, even if in theory.

Before Neil Armstrong landed on the moon, few people believed it was possible. However, a team of U.S. scientists knew that it would work in theory. To this end, they designed the Apollo missions that went to the moon. The rest is history. As long as your outcome has a basis in reality or theoretical feasibility, it is realistic.

Timed ✓

Make sure your outcome is *timed* by attaching a specific deadline to its accomplishment. I often ask people what their dreams are and as they start to glow with euphoria, they describe them to me in perfect detail. Later on in the conversation, I inevitably ask them what their goals are: immediate, short-term, and long-term. Their goals, if any, are radically different and do not bear any resemblance to their dreams. Their dreams are what they really want. Those dreams are unlikely to be achieved unless there is a deadline attached along with a workable plan on how to achieve them.

Goals are dreams with deadlines. Impotent goals do nothing for one's motivation. That is why it is so important to have an outcome for this book and by when you want to achieve your specific, measurable results. A good example is, "By the time I finish this book, after I gain unstoppable confidence, I will be able to walk up to any stranger and introduce myself." Another good example is, "I will feel warm and relaxed when talking to strangers in social situations."

Monitor Your Progress Throughout This Book

A key to achieving SMART outcomes is to *monitor your progress*. Be accountable to yourself and check in periodically, to notice your results as consistently and frequently as you wish. No one needs to give you permission to accomplish all of your outcomes, achieve all of your goals, and live your dreams. You can do that right now! Each time you get the results you want, stop for a moment and congratulate yourself. Treat yourself somehow to something extraordinary. If you find that you are not yet getting the results you want, step back and look at what you can do differently. Keep doing things differently, adjusting your path until you get what you want.

Gaining more confidence is a process rather than a single event. For each different area of our lives, we can expand our comfort zones further. Whatever level of confidence you have, you can always have more. The techniques presented in this book will give you the tools for expanding your confidence for the rest of your life.

Reclaiming Your Dreams

The process of gaining confidence means we should also reclaim our dreams. This means going back into your past and reclaiming your passions. Find what you REALLY love to do…what it is that fires you up…what is so magnificent that you want to do…think about what excites you in the world…as you do that…you can become aware that you can *reconnect* with that passion. Everybody that told you that it wasn't possible was talking about *their **own** limits*. It only means that it wasn't possible for them. Their limits are their own and not yours! It's all about finding your dreams. It's been said that most people die when they are 35 yet they are not buried until they are in their 70s. Because at this point, 35, perhaps trapped in a job they hate, locked into their lifestyle, mortgage, having not gone after their dream…yet they still can…and that is what this book is about. Take these techniques and use them to fulfill your dreams.

How This Book Differs From Other Self-Help Books

This book differs from the other self-help books on the shelf because it is not about theory. It is about doing what works. It is about finding what has worked for others who are confident, figuring out how to do that, and then doing it yourself. Many of the fluff motivation books on the market remind me of someone blowing up a balloon really big and then letting it go. We both know what happens to the balloon. It flies all around the room aimlessly until it returns to its original, shriveled up shape and stays back on the ground. Filling yourself up with motivation is great, yet motivation must ultimately come from within. There is a difference between someone telling you to "GO FOR IT!" and someone telling you to "GO FOR IT!" and *also* giving you the specific tools to do exactly that.

This book is not based upon theory. This is based on what works. I'm on the street, trying this stuff out and learning from my mistakes. The beauty of this book is that you can learn from the mistakes I made in the course of doing whatever it took to get unstoppable confidence and prosper from my knowledge. You can take what works from this book and use it in your life. Discard what you do not. Some techniques you'll like, some you may not, and some you will love. Don't just take my word that these techniques really work. This is not gospel. Do the techniques and prove it to yourself.

The techniques discussed in this book are no-nonsense, street-tested, immediately applicable tools for your empowerment. I'll give you specific instructions on how and when to use these tools in your life. These techniques are so effective because they take what has worked, what does work, and what will work and breaks it down into small, learnable strategies that you can use to help yourself. When you learn those same strategies, you will be able to duplicate the same results. At the same time, we throw away the useless techniques that have kept us stuck. We will go over the techniques that keep people stuck, too, so we can notice if we are engaging in one of those activities and immediately shift gears.

If you are looking for pie-in-the-sky theory, put this book down immediately! If you want to wade through a jargon-filled muddle, stop reading right now. If you want academic techniques that work only sometimes and only if you follow complicated procedures, you will not find them here.

Now that you know how to use this book, realize that **the key to this book is *action*.** As the phrase goes, "the proper fruit of knowledge is action" and this is absolutely true. Anything else is unacceptable. This book is about getting you results: real, tangible results in all areas of your life.

Beyond Positive Thinking

Positive thinking is an excellent technique and revolutionary for its time. The problem is that if someone sits around all day thinking positively without really solving their problems, their life is really not better off, is it? People can think positively but when we empower them with tools on how to get their goals and solve their problems, this is much more effective.

Positive thinking was good for its time, and we have Dr. Norman Vincent Peale to thank for popularizing this idea. He proposed that if you think positively you will get the results you want, and this can be true in some cases.

Now we are in the 21st Century. We have made huge leaps in our understanding of human functioning and performance, and while we salute the pioneers, we must move with the times and take the opportunity to avail ourselves of cutting-edge technology. Let's take Dr. Peale's excellent results and apply them where possible and add on to them even further. We can crank it to the max.

It is vital to remember that *positive thinking without action is useless*. All the motivation that you will get in this book will not do you any good unless you take action. It's not true motivation until you take action. If you only get hyped up and inspired without taking action to change your life, it's no different from someone who is not motivated at all. It's like the phrase, "The person who does not read is no better off than the person who can't." For our purposes, we can think of the phrase as, "The person who has knowledge and does not apply it is no better off than the person who is ignorant."

The Problem With Affirmations In A Vacuum

Sometimes people have the tendency to overly rely on affirmations. They'll say the affirmations over and over without anything else. The problem with affirmations in a vacuum is that you won't gain the full results. Couple affirmations with the techniques presented in this book and you have a recipe for unlocking the unstoppable you.

This book is designed to be practical and immediately usable. You should be able to apply these techniques the first time you read them. This is no-nonsense stuff. I've stripped away all the jargon and all the fluff because there is an unstoppable person inside you waiting to be unleashed.

Affirmations have a place as well and they will be discussed later on in this book. An important thing about affirmations is that they do not work as a stand-alone tool. Chanting some mantra over and over again helps drill the belief into your unconscious mind, and while that is helpful and useful in some contexts, that alone will not get you where you want to go.

My Journey To Unstoppable Confidence

My Shy Self: The High-School Years

I had always been shy as a child and even as a young adult. I had a small, select group of close friends my entire life yet never found enough confidence to introduce myself to a stranger. This led to serious difficulties for me in dating and relating with women. My friends and I excelled in school and that was our main focus yet in the back of my mind I knew I was missing out on something else when all the other people in high school were going out on dates and hanging around one another. I thought to myself that I must be different or that something must be wrong with me. Consequently, I found myself rationalizing that I could do that if I chose to but my main area to excel at and concentrate on was school.

However, deep down, I secretly desired to trade places with some of the other kids just to experience what it was like to go on a date or to be comfortable with someone of the opposite sex. The more I thought about how much fun they were having hanging out and having normal teenage experiences, the worse I felt about myself. It was as if I had the inability to really connect to another person at a deep level. Searching for a way to escape, I turned to studying even harder and burying myself in my books. At that time, it was all I knew how to do. Now, in reflection, one can easily realize that there are other choices available to someone at all times. We always have options and it's important to be able to recognize as many options as possible and then naturally decide for ourselves which option suits us best.

In four years of high school, I went on exactly one date. Of course, it wasn't me who initiated it. The girl approached me after class one day and asked me if I wanted to hang out with her one night. Smiling broadly and trying to contain my overwhelming enthusiasm at this seemingly incredible, unprecedented event, I gladly accepted. Later on in the week, she called me and we set the date for the following Friday.

She picked me up and we went to a local fast-food restaurant. All throughout dinner, the conversation was strained as she tried her best to pry me from my shy shell. Every time I began to come out of the shell, I automatically retreated back into the shell simply because of my dreadful shy habit. She did her absolute best to talk with me and have a good time. Still, I could tell she saw my shyness as an obstacle to getting to know one another. My saving grace for the date was that I would smile a lot and reciprocate all questions she asked me. The conversation went better as long as she did the talking.

After finishing dinner, she drove us up to a mountainous lookout point with a beautiful view of the city. She asked me for suggestions on what I wanted to do but I was too shy to suggest anything for fear of "rejection." It was a clear night with the stars illuminating the sky. I didn't really understand what this gesture meant. Later, I learned from other high school friends that the spot we went to was the designated spot to have a great kissing session. While I was able to maintain good eye contact with the young lady, sometimes there were pauses in the conversations that of course seemed like eternity to me. And at these times, my internal dialogue came alive as if it were an annoying younger sibling whose life mission is to prevent you from enjoying yourself.

"What if I have some gunk in my teeth? Does she want me to kiss her? If I kiss her, how should I do that? Does she really like me? Is she bored of me? What should I say next? Why are we really here? What does it mean? What should I do next? Do I look at the stars outside the car with her? Should I hold her hand? My goodness, she sure is pretty. Is she noticing me turning red with embarrassment? How come I'm so darn shy? Do I want to kiss her? When should I do it?"

The internal dialogue continued on and on like that for the entire night. No wonder I could not hold a conversation with her. How could I when I was so busy having a conversation with myself? None of my attention could be left over to talk with her. After an hour more of forced conversation, she finally dropped me off at home and extended her hand to offer a handshake in lieu of repeating one of the previous awkward episodes.

Through the high school gossip grapevine, I found out that the woman had recently broken up with her long-term boyfriend and immediately called to ask me out. And I wondered if it was really a coincidence that we went to the same restaurant he worked at. Was she hoping he'd be there? The ultimate conclusion for me was that she was just trying to make him jealous and have him find out about our 'date' even though she did seem interested in me. But if I discount that 'date', that brings me to zero dates for all of high school. That seems about right and proportional for how shy I was.

I share this miserable tale of shyness to let you know that no matter how shy or confident you are now, you can improve and become more confident. Unfortunately, I was the shyest guy in the world during my high school days. People attributed my inaction and unwillingness to initiate activities with others as being antisocial, aloof, indecisive, reactive, and generally unfriendly. What I found most painful was that I wanted to be social, proactive, decisive, and friendly only at that time I did not know how. That was the most frustrating part was being as if I were trapped in a shell and unable to be who I really was all along. This book is designed to allow you to be more of who you already are and be comfortable with yourself in the presence of others.

My Shy Self: The College Years

Now, as you've read about my ultra-shyness in high school, you may be thinking that it couldn't get any worse. It did. Since I was so good at being shy, I really outdid myself in college. The more the years passed the more I found my inability to be confident to be a glaring weakness.

My roommates meant well when they would try to get me to drink to loosen up. Their hearts were in the right spot. God bless them! They knew I was "stiff" and very shy. Instead of hanging out with them and drinking and socializing, I would spend my time on the computer, chatting with strangers through electronic mail. How could I turn down the opportunity to hang out with my friends and instead chat with strangers halfway around the world? I rationalized it by saying I did not do that since I didn't drink. I didn't know I could still hang out with them and socialize with them while I was not drinking. That option, easily the most obvious choice now, never even crossed my mind.

One night, after a few too many beers, my roommates and their friends spotted me screwing around on the computer and set it about as their mission to get me to loosen up. Their mission henceforth was to get me drunk as a skunk. They proceeded to apply some very persuasive peer pressure and invited me upstairs where a party was being held. Being flattered that they even recognized me, I finally said yes and resolutely stated that I would not drink though. After getting upstairs and getting into the midst of the party, one of my giving roommates handed me an "orange juice" and said to drink up. At this point in time, I chugged it. The next thing you know, I was feeling tipsy and really relaxed as I noticed myself automatically talking more and having lots more fun. In my semi-drunken stupor, I realized that the orange juice contained alcohol. However, I was finally feeling good and accepted so I chose to drink some more. It was my first experience with alcohol. And I found that I quite liked being able to drink to the point of obvious inebriation since it temporarily allowed me to relax and stop being shy. At this point in time, you may or may not be thinking whether one of the Unstoppable Confidence techniques is to get sloshed and drown out your shyness with alcohol. The answer is no. It's just at that time, I didn't realize there were other ways to overcome one's shyness.

After that great first drinking experience, I decided I liked it and did it a lot more. When the weekend came, I talked to a number of people to find where "the party" was being held. Once at the party, I proceeded to get seriously drunk. My faulty logic was, "If one beer is good, then that means two beers are better." Following this faulty logic had me drunk in no time. And simultaneously, I transformed myself from being a shy wallflower who spoke to no one to being a raving, whirling dervish of a humorous drunk who spoke to people, told jokes, laughed loud and long, and had a great time. It was at these parties that my friends had to tell me it was time to go home but I never wanted to leave. This was my escape from my shy self and I wanted it to last as long as I could. I needed it to last as long as I could. That was why I would metaphorically pretend I was a doctor and prescribed alcohol to myself as a self-medication for my shyness.

As a result of these parties, I woke up in strange places, forgot what I had done the previous night when I was drunk, and felt miserable with a hangover. Still, in my mind, drinking was my ticket out of shyness. What I hadn't realized was that I had other options. Without other options to be more confident, I did the best I could with what I knew. And that, unfortunately, was to drink to excess.

One day after having a miserable hangover, I crossed my threshold. I said, "STOP!" inside my mind. I decided that there had to be another way. After all, I had seen other people who behaved confidently without resorting to getting smashed-down drunk. I decided I'd find out what they were doing. This meant that I found myself reading a number of self-help books. From each of these self-help books, I gained a little knowledge or a useful exercise to enhance my confidence in myself and allow me to relax in the presence of others.

This book is a collection of everything useful I've read in the books, experienced in my life, or have modeled from other confident people. By doing these exercises, you will gain the confidence that you seek. After you get the confidence you want, you'll be able to look back on this as the starting point of your confident journey with life as an amazing adventure.

My Search For Solutions

I began searching for answers. Finally, I guaranteed myself that I would become confident in whatever I wanted to do. I *will* gain confidence. Ultimately, it was the experience of my breaking out of my shell that gave me the confidence. For me, it was talking to women. I decided that I would approach every single woman I saw! At first, I would simply smile at them. And you know what? They responded. Not all of them, but enough to encourage me to expand my comfort zone a little further. This small success catapulted me to the next step in me expanding my comfort zone. Next, I would approach women and simply say "Hi." Again, this slight widening of my comfort zone encouraged me. After all, I was an adult and had to take care of my confidence myself.

I had two choices. I could either retreat back to my comfort zone and be shy, blaming someone else for making me that way. Or I could take responsibility and go for it. When my confidence really grew, I got to the point where I could meet women and gain instant rapport with them, conversing with them at ease. You'll learn the techniques I use later in this book.

One specific example of my being painfully shy was with a woman at my college named Allison. She was breathtaking, tall, thin, and athletic. She intrigued me. I would walk by her and smile to her. She smiled back at me, too. For other men with more confidence, they naturally would have taken this as a signal to approach her. I knew what I wanted to do, I knew what I should do (approach her), I just didn't know how. And it was extremely frustrating. I was literally paralyzed with fear and incapacitated. I would go to all of her volleyball games just to watch her play. She was awesome. I wanted to talk to her so badly since I had a huge crush on her. When I look back on it, I think it's too bad I did not have the confidence to talk. Fortunately, I have the confidence now and you will too by the time you finish reading this book and doing the exercises.

Confidence In Contexts

We all have a comfort zone, a set of things we feel comfortable doing. It varies in each area of our lives. An air traffic controller may be calm, cool, and collected while he has hundreds of lives at stake. Now, on the road, with his teenager learning how to drive the family car, he could easily panic because he has a different comfort zone. Our challenge is to perpetually expand this comfort zone, doing new and different things. This means that we are evolving and growing. The beauty of expanding your comfort zone is that there is a certain rush when you do it. There is this surge of energy, this rush you feel when you do something new. You feel really alive. Especially coming out on the other side of something that maybe you weren't sure you could do and realize how successfully you did it, you feel good, don't you? And you look back and casually remark, "It wasn't such a big deal after all."

This rush of vitality in expanding your comfort zone can be addictive! We all have addictions. People can be addicted to anything in the world. People can be addicted to negative things: alcohol, drugs, gambling, sex, etc. If you stop and think about it, if people can make addictions in the negative sense, what stops us from becoming positively addicted? It's a revelation to understand that you can aim your addictions in the right direction. What if you were to aim your addictions to health, vitality, achieving goals, and expanding your comfort zone? I'm addicted to increasing my comfort zone and I'm the first to admit it. Always ask yourself, "What is new and different? What can I do differently?" That rush that I feel from expanding my comfort zone has me hooked. We can all experience this same rush when we expand our comfort zones. You could say that becoming addicted to stepping outside your comfort zone is what life is about. Growing. Changing. Evolving.

Beginning To Run Your Own Brain For A Change

The Myth Of The Shy Gene

So up until now, how have you thought of yourself? Were you shy? Were you tentative? That's how some people label themselves, which brings me to the myth of "That's just the way I am." What a loaded phrase. Are you confident? Are you shy? Are you tentative? They say, "That's just the way I am." They need to stop saying that. It's as if they are chanting a negatively reinforcing mantra. The real secret is that it's a dirty, rotten, broken affirmation that keeps people stuck. The affirmation "Every day and every way I'm getting better and better" is a famous affirmation by Emile Coue, an early self-help pioneer. "I'm shy because that's the way I am" will work as an affirmation also if people repeat it. If others repeat this phrase, append to their statement, "They are shy because that's just the way they are *according to them*." That myth is the worst myth ever passed on from disempowered people to other disempowered people.

Believing that your parents were shy and caused you to be shy is no excuse. Same goes for your kids. People do not become shy automatically when they are born. There is no 'shyness gene.' Shy people can't blame their genes. People become shy because they've learned to behave and act in a certain way. When I was shy around people, it's because I was in the habit of looking at a person, saying inside my mind, "He/she won't like me," and then feeling bad inside, picturing him/her rejecting me, and then feeling immense fear that paralyzed me. That was simply the way I learned to behave. I only knew one way of behaving, but fortunately I got more choices. Kids unconsciously pick up the behaviors of the parents. Your parents may have influenced you to be shy, but that's different from them inflicting you with some untreatable genetic disease, which is really what it really means when people say, "That's just the way I am!"

Let me tell you about the myth of "I'm shy." It's an excuse and enables people to stay stuck. Shyness is not a trait; it's only a way of acting. If you can act one way that means you can act another way, too. Shy is a behavior; it's not an adjective that describes a person. It's not a state of being. It's a way of acting. You can behave in a confident manner, too. You always have that choice. People locked into the "I'm shy" method don't realize they have the choice.

Consider this: if you could choose your identity, if you could choose the way you see yourself, then would you deliberately label yourself as shy? As a person lacking confidence? As hesitant or introverted or *anything* less than glorious? Absolutely not. And yet, that's unfortunately what so many people do when they say, "I'm shy, I'm just not confident," or anything else of that nature.

Therefore, it's important to avoid the phrase "I'm shy."

Worse than saying "I'm shy" is talking about shyness as if it's some sort of disease or disorder. "Yeah, he has a case of shyness." "She has a case of shyness disorder." That is the most ridiculous thing ever. If I walk into a room of shy people and there's this bug that flies around and it bites me, do I become shy, too? No. That is downright absurd. People don't go walking along one day and go "UGH!" and crumple to the ground, and suddenly they are diagnosed with shyness.

Since it's not a disorder, we're in luck. Few people realize that we have all the resources we need to behave in a confident manner, and as this realization sinks in to you now, you can feel really good, knowing how radically you will change yourself. You can choose to behave in a confident manner. In the case of confidence, it's useful to think of confidence as contagious and infectious. The confidence bug can bite you. It may not be absolutely true, yet it's useful to believe. In fact, this book contains a very potent species of confidence bugs and they will bite you all throughout this book. There is a powerful frame of mind at work here:

It's the *"as if"* frame.

The "As If" Frame

If you act *as if* something is real for long enough, you will eventually forget that you are only pretending, and however you are acting will become your habit. People who used to be shy have used this *"as if"* frame of mind to develop their confidence. The difference between people who are confident and those who are shy is their habits.

Habits can either be good or bad. The secret is to have good habits. The more empowering habits you have, the better your life will be. Developing these habits of behaving confidently is enjoyable, too. It's exciting to witness your personal transformation as you gain more confidence in yourself.

The Pretend It And Have It Technique

The mind and body are part of a cybernetic system. This means that the body influences the mind and the mind influences the body. We can pretend to have confidence by reliving confident experiences in our mind, and our body will adopt confident physiology. Or if we choose to adopt confident physiology, our mind will adjust what you are seeing, hearing, and feeling internally to experience confidence. We can use this to our advantage. You can pretend anything and master it. Getting confidence is no different than that. You can pretend to have confidence and pretty soon you'll forget that you're pretending and by the time you've done that, your habitual confidence is a habit. Following that, your confidence gets ingrained into you as a person when you think about yourself as a confident person.

Remember times in your past when you played "make-believe" as a child? Children have excellent imaginations and are very good at playing and consequently learning. Pretend that you have the confidence before you really do have it. If you were to be ten times more confident than you are now, answer the following questions:

- How would you be moving differently right now?
- How would your body posture be different right now?
- How would you be talking to yourself inside differently right now?
- How would you be speaking to others right now?

- What do you see inside your mind to instantly make you ten times more confident right now?
- What do you hear inside your mind to instantly make you ten times more confident right now?
- What kind of confident feeling in your body would you experience?
- Where in your body would you feel that confidence first?
- How could you intensify that confident feeling in your body?

In answering the questions and doing what the questions presuppose you will do, your unstoppable confidence will soar. When your confidence soars, forget that you're pretending and follow through on taking action to do whatever you need to get done.

I've used this technique a lot when I first learned how to walk up and begin talking to strangers. I would ask myself all of the questions listed above and then answer them one by one. With each question I answered, I adjusted my behavior to pretend as if I already had the confidence I was seeking. And after I had finished answering all the questions, I actually could feel unstoppable confidence within me. This propelled me to go introduce myself to some strangers and begin talking to them.

The reverse is also true, so be forewarned about that. If you think about shyness and adopt shy body language, your mind and body will make you feel shy. If you catch yourself doing this, acknowledge it and then begin asking yourself the confidence questions designed to get you into a super confident state.

Confident and shy body language (physiology) differ greatly. Having shy body language means hanging your head as if you're ashamed of yourself, slumping your shoulders forward, having a droopy back instead of standing up straight, and looking down to the ground. Having confident body language means keeping your head held high, your shoulders back, your abdominal muscles tucked in, standing up tall and proud. By realizing the difference, you can be sure to maintain confident body language as you have unstoppable confidence.

Do You Run Your Mind?

Ask yourself, "Who runs your mind?" Now, before you have a knee-jerk reaction and answer, "I do," you have to become aware of who and what is influencing you. Do you watch TV? Do you program yourself with the mass media? They don't call it TV 'programming' for no reason at all! Who else do you allow to influence you? Who you hang out with is who you become. Friends adopt traits of friends.

Most people I meet are living what I term "accidental lifestyles." They allow ✓
external influences and circumstances to randomly lead them to whatever
lifestyle they are living. Contrast this with a purposeful, goal-directed lifestyle
where everything is designed. People who are living the lives of their dreams
are doing that by design. It does not happen accidentally; you have to *make* ✓
it happen. Realize that you and only you have complete control over your
own thoughts. Any emotion that you experience that causes you to take
action or that keeps you incapacitated is an emotion that you have given
power. People are *not* helpless automatons floating through space respond-
ing to everything without any choices. You can choose which emotions to
give power to, and which to leave behind.

The Origins Of A Lack Of Confidence

Lack of confidence comes from a number of areas: society, parents, schools,
and the media. We'll examine how this happens and how if you have children,
you can prevent this from happening to them. You'll install unstoppable confidence in them.

In many ways, society conditions people to "go with the flow," to "accept what
is offered," and "don't make any waves." Sometimes, this is falsely interpreted
by some as advice to NOT follow their dreams. If you need to step outside of
what is normal and usual to pursue your dreams, then do exactly that.

Parents

Parents can be major contributors to a lack of confidence. Throughout life, their ✓₂
purpose is to teach the child and draw the child out to experience their full
potential, to be who they were meant to be. Yet sometimes parents strip away
the child's individuality and inadvertently instill limits in the child. Parents often
try to get kids to conform to the view of what they think is correct.

How many times have you heard the following phrases?

- "Act like a grownup."
- "Act your age."
- "Stop acting childish." (as if that is a bad thing)
- "Be realistic."
- "Get your head out of the clouds."
- "He's such a dreamer."
- "That's a crazy idea."
- "I've never heard of anything like that before."
- "No one has ever done that before."

Parents always have a positive intention motivating their every behavior, yet sometimes they don't always communicate that. Take the phrase "Act like a grownup." What does that mean? To have all the limits most adults do, to not play and experience pure joy like a child, to not learn, wonder, or explore? If that were acting like a grownup, I'd rather pass. Or consider the phrase "Stop acting childish." The notion of exploring, laughing a lot, and learning a lot is really what life is all about and kids have the right idea. It is completely the natural state of humans. What about the notion of being "realistic"? What does that really mean? Realistic according to whom? How specifically should I be realistic? The phrase is ludicrous. Calling people dreamers or telling people to get their head out of the clouds does not help people. It's not helpful at all. It only instills limits in them and tries to bring them back into the bound of what is socially acceptable.

School

School has a huge influence over children. We're mandated to go. Teachers are powerful authority figures and peer pressure is extremely high. We're taught to fit in. Everyone wants to fit in. How does school create a lack of confidence? One factor is peer pressure. The kids make fun of one another if anyone does anything differently. School also divides kids into different learning tracks, which is most unfortunate. Mathematics is an example: high, medium, low math learners. Kids are intelligent, smarter than which we typically give them credit. They understand these labels and they integrate them into their identities. The students labeled "slow" integrate this into themselves as a belief, "I stink at math." And their beliefs create their reality and way of being. The top performers perform to their expectations. The medium ones perform moderately. The poor performers perform poorly. They perform exactly how they are expected and taught to perform.

A research study in the 1960s showed how powerfully expectation influences performance. One teacher was told her set of students was exceptional, but in reality it was really a standard cross-section of students. This "exceptional" class performed exceptionally that year, and the teacher commented on how eager the students were to learn, and how much she enjoyed teaching them. The next year, another normal cross-section of students were in her class. This time, the experimenters told her that these students were poor performers. As expectation and beliefs create reality, the "poor" students performed awfully. The same teacher, who had just had the "exceptional" students the prior year, remarked how awful the students were, how they hated learning, and how hard they were to teach. We can take this same idea and project only positive expectations onto our own children. Furthermore, we can expect excellence from all people we interact with. You will surprise yourself at how often people will rise up to whatever standards you set for them.

The Media

The media is another source from which a lack of confidence comes. The mainstream media is funded by advertising, and ultimately is out to get people to consume. TV is "free" because advertisers take large amounts of money in order to get TV to show their product to the captive audience. Radio is free for the same reason. Individuality is dangerous to these advertisers because when you think for yourself, you can decide for yourself whether the product is right for you or not. You won't be buying for the sake of conforming and for the sake of "keeping up with the Joneses." It is their benefit if you lack confidence. They use tactics such as showing how everyone else exactly like you has the product and therefore you must need it as well. They teach you to feel bad if you don't have their product. They teach you that life can become an instant party if you consume their products.

My favorite example of this is in the stereotypical beer commercial. You watch a less than healthy guy watching TV endlessly and see him given a beer. You already know what happens next, at least according to the commercial. Life instantly becomes a party, beautiful women swoon over him, and he realizes he has his dream sports car, he is vacationing on a tropical island, and he can forget about any of life's ordinary troubles. It behooves the media to do this to sell more products.

Learning To Be Confident From Kids

Have you ever watched a kid play? They really know how to dig in and thoroughly enjoy what they are doing. They totally embrace what they are doing. Kids are true dreamers. It's a tragedy that this is socially conditioned out of them through the various influences discussed earlier. Some people say, "Kids say the craziest things." Why do they do that? They do that because kids realize anything is possible. Kids are natural dreamers. Too often, adults say, "That can't be done" or "Be realistic." Children, in essence, have not learned to be limited like adults have.

In fact, when we are born, we enter this world with only two natural fears:

1. The fear of falling.
2. The fear of loud noises.

Aside from the fear of falling and the fear of loud noises, all other fears are learned. Human beings are magnificent at learning. Because you have learned to fear other things aside from the only two natural fears, you can naturally empower yourself to move past your fear by learning new ways of behaving.

A study was conducted among adults to research what was their greatest fear, and the fear of public speaking rated higher than the fear of death. This is irrational and doesn't make any sense. Being more afraid of public speaking than death is a direct result of learning to fear something that does not need to be feared. Fear can be characterized by the acronym F.E.A.R., meaning False Evidence Appearing Real. When people realize that public speaking is simply a process and not a life-or-death event, the false evidence disappears and with it goes the fear. With the fear gone, people can be their naturally confident selves.

Confidence As Our Natural State Of Being

A state of confidence is really our natural state of being. The fact is that when we're born we are simply not self-conscious. It's not like we pop out of the womb and go, "Oh, I'm naked. Could somebody please get me some clothes here? Oooohhh, I'm shy now! Oh no, everybody's looking at me and I'm naked!" That example is completely ludicrous. Children are already in their natural state of being absolutely confident, full of wonder, and ready to explore the world around them. What if we were to adopt that same child-like attitude for going after what we wanted in the world?

When you were a baby, did you immediately pop out of the womb and stand up and start walking around just like it was completely normal to you? Obviously, you did not. Neither did I. No one did. In learning how to walk, children take the attitude, "Hey, I'm going to do this walking thing. I see others around me doing it and I know I can do it, too. I'm going to persevere. It doesn't matter how many times I fall down. It only matters that I keep getting up." If you get the chance, watch kids as they begin to walk. They crawl around, stand up, wobble around, fall down and then do it all over again. Kids continue doing this until they learn how to consistently walk. Nothing will stop them from learning how to walk. When you have this same attitude in going after your goals, nothing will stop you from achieving them.

What if kids were infected with the same less-than-useful attitudes that some adults have that state, "If we try something and it doesn't work, we just give up"? We'd have all these people who refuse to walk just because they didn't get it down perfectly when they were kids. They tried it once and it didn't work so they gave up. They decided they weren't walkers. Can you picture a little baby with his arms crossed, pouting, scowling intensely just because it took the less-than-resourceful adult attitude that "If something doesn't immediately work, then that means it's time to give up"? Can you imagine a little baby saying in a snooty manner, "Walking isn't for me! I do other things. I've tried it once. It's really not all that it's cut out to be." Fortunately, kids keep on going and going until they master the skills. We as adults can learn from them and keep the same attitudes that children have toward learning.

Hypersensitivity As A Cause Of Shyness

Sometimes being overly sensitive in terms of feelings can lead to shyness. People can become afraid of doing anything for fear of offending someone, hurting someone else's feelings, or getting in trouble. Being supersensitive may be useful in some contexts, such as when you want to really empathize with a person, yet if a person is supersensitive all the time then that is detrimental. I know this because I used to be hypersensitive. I never spoke up, never stepped outside my comfort zone, and never did anything that might have the remotest possibility of aggravating people. This occurred as a result of my incapacitating fear. I figured that since I was so sensitive, with such thin skin, others must be the same way so I needed to tiptoe around everyone so as to manage their feelings. What nonsense I later discovered this to be.

It's important to be sensitive to a point, yet you need to have confidence to ✓ do what it takes to achieve your outcome at the same time. People are ✓ remarkably resilient. If you have confidence and accidentally hurt someone's feelings, there's a very simple remedy. You apologize, resolve not to do that again, and move on. It's really very simple. Understanding this means a whole world of new options unlocked for you because you can be, do, and have anything you want. Go for it. If there is trouble or if someone is offended, you have all the resources you need to handle it.

Confidence Is A Process

Let me let you in on a little secret. Confidence is not a thing. It's not something you eat, drink, or inject into yourself. It's none of that. By calling something confidence, it's actually a misnomer. There is only such thing as acting confident or behaving in a confident way. There isn't a confidence pill you take to become confident in whatever you do. Someone who behaves in a confident manner is said to have confidence. Someone who behaves in a tentative manner is said to lack confidence. And confidence is context dependent. Confidence isn't pervasive everywhere in all facets. You don't catch it like a disease. It's simply a process that you do inside your mind.

The same goes for any emotion, be it fear, sadness, depression or anxiety. None of these are actual 'things.' They are the result of processes, *sequences* ✓✓ *of thought* that you run in your mind. Up until now, you may not have been ✓ aware that you were doing this, and the vital thing to realize is that *you* have complete control over these processes. You can decide which mental ✓ processes have use and which do not, and if they are useless, you can stop, interrupt and banish them.

Let's begin now to blow out those negative emotions. A great place to begin ✓✓ to interrupt and banish those useless thought processes is to **consider the**

language you use to describe them. Let's say you've feared public speaking. How do you *describe* this to yourself? If you say,"I have a fear of speaking in public" you are, in a sense, taking possession of something that is just a mental process! What if you were to describe what is really happening and say,"When I think about a certain context, I run a process in my mind which I have labeled as 'fear'." How much does that change things for you? How much better do you feel, knowing that what you previously described as "a fear of public speaking" is really just a process you ran in your mind?

Begin now to notice how you have been describing your other negative emotions. Have you been saying things like,"I always get nervous when I talk to strangers","Talking to customers makes me anxious,""I just feel depressed,"?

∨ Instead of feeling,"I feel sad", describe for yourself what is really going on:"I choose to think in a certain way that results in my feeling 'sad' when I encounter a certain set of circumstances." It may sound a bit hokey at first, but as you think about it, really think about the meaning of that sentence, you will begin to gain a sense of how truly liberating this is.

∨ By changing your language, you change your life.

The language you use to describe what you are feeling impacts that feeling tremendously, and it is your knowledge, your awareness of these processes that gives you power over them. Just like when somebody says, "I'm depressed."What they've done here is built that notion into their very being. Nobody can be depressed all the time. If they were, they wouldn't call it depression. It'd just be their normal state of being. Instead, people who consider themselves depressed should be saying,"I run a process through my mind that causes me to experience certain pictures, sounds, and feelings inside that I have collectively labeled as depression." The same goes for anxiety.

Now, after taking control of these processes, put a good emotion in place of the negative emotion."I have absolute confidence in public speaking." Try that out. The negative processes do not serve you. If you catch yourself running one of these negative processes, interrupt it! Inside your mind, go FFFFFFFFTTTT....wait a minute....STOP! Make the sound inside your mind...DING...stop the negative process. Start the resourceful process. As

∨ you go through your day, become aware of what you are seeing, hearing, and thinking inside yourself and realize that **you have control**. Change your physiology to have a confident state. Change your internal pictures, your internal voice, to suit you.

∨ Congratulate yourself when you stop the negative processes and praise yourself when you start a confident process, because you get more of what you reinforce. Praising yourself gives you incentive to run the resourceful process. Naturally, you'll then be more likely to do it again in the future. After all, you should treat yourself well. Some people have negative internal voices nagging at them all day. How awful would it be to live like that? Remember, the only person who you spend all your time with is yourself. You may as well have great rapport with yourself. Compliment yourself. Praise yourself. Just do it. When you do something well, congratulate yourself. Similarly, do that whenever you step outside your comfort zone. Celebrate those successes and reward yourself accordingly!

Consider the example of the rookie salesperson, Janet. Janet finds herself saying, "Talking to customers is scary. They frighten me and I feel the fear when I go to ask them to purchase my product. I just don't know what to do."

What is occurring here is that Janet has give up her personal power by using disempowering language. If we were to reword her language in such a way that would allow her to easily change her perception of the situation, the translation would be, "According to me, right now, talking to customers causes me to experience a certain emotion that I describe as scary. I choose to allow them to frighten me and I do something inside my mind that collectively I label as fear, which I then feel while I ask them to purchase my product. I don't know what to do yet."

Here is what Janet can do to immediately gain control over her emotions:

1. Append "according to me at this time" onto every sentence of hers. This forces her to acknowledge that what she is describing is not absolute truth and not etched in stone for all time.

2. Whenever there is an unwanted emotion (e.g., fear, guilt, anxiety), she must pre-append the emotion with the following phrase: "I choose to experience a certain emotion by doing something inside my mind, which causes me to experience a set of pictures, sounds, and feelings that I collectively have labeled…" [Emotion] This requires Janet to take the fixed emotion and turn it back into a process, which it already was all the time. It also demonstrates to her that she is the one doing the process. Since she is the one doing the process, that means that she obviously has control over it.

3. When she catches herself using that disempowered language, after she restates it using the guidelines above, she must empower herself by using sentences stating how she will behave in the future. An example is, "Although I've done that **in the past,** I wonder how quickly I will find myself becoming more relaxed and confident when I go to ask the customers to purchase my product."

As you've gone through this example and seen how it's done, and read the step-by-step account of how to do it yourself, you now realize you can do it now. In fact, it's now time for you to think of five unwanted emotions and a context in which you experience those emotions. While you do that, become cognizant of the language you are using to describe what you really do to experience those unwanted emotions, and think of emotions that would best fit in their place after you rid yourself of them. Following that, do the exercise of changing your language and adding in more empowered language. Remember that when you change your language, you change your life. Throughout this book, you'll be learning many more effective and simple ways to use language, and many more mental processes that will give you *warp-speed* confidence.

Releasing The Past

If you would, think about how you were in your past. Who cares if you were shy, or if you weren't confident in the way you wanted to be in the past? The past is the past. There's nothing we can really do about it now; the best thing we can do is learn from it and behave differently in the future. To that extent, I want you to forgive yourself, your former self, for being shy and not acting confidently in the past. So often people spend their valuable time and energy kicking themselves for time and opportunities they lost as a consequence of being shy. So stop now and before you read any further, if you were unconfident in the past, if you were shy or whatever, forgive yourself now. Release all those feelings of negativity or any frustration or anything bad you might have toward being shy in the past, because that is a thing of the past. We're going to learn from it and we're going to move on.

If you catch people trying to define you as shy, now that you've practiced these exercises, now that you're discovering your new-found confidence, I want you to swiftly and politely correct them, saying , "No, that's the way I used to behave as a shy person. I'm now confident. Thank you very much." Not only should this be all it takes for this person to get the message and to stop trying to impose old limits onto you, but, in fact, they will welcome the new, confident you.

Levels Of Competence

There are four different levels of competence that people go through as they develop any skill. Those four levels are: unconscious incompetence, conscious incompetence, conscious competence, and unconscious competence. You will travel through these stages as you reach unstoppable confidence.

Unconscious Incompetence

Unconscious incompetence means that we do not possess a skill and aren't even aware how useful that skill could be to us. Someone who is extremely shy and who does not even recognize how beneficial learning how to be more confident would be to them could be considered unconsciously incompetent in the area of confidence.

I spent the first twenty years of my life like this. Being shy, I neither knew no other way of being nor was I cognizant of the fact that people don't have to live trapped in shy shells. By reading this book, you have already passed through this stage of unconscious incompetence. Picking up this book means you are looking for a better way to live, which means you're at least at the next stage (or perhaps further) on your unstoppable confidence journey.

Conscious Incompetence

When I was in college, when I finally looked around and realized just how shy I was and that other people were actually confident, I moved to the second level of skill development, which is that of *conscious incompetence.* I became aware of just how shy I was. When we become aware of something lacking in our lives, that is a great opportunity since it means we get a chance to improve our lives. When I became conscious of my incompetence, I began reading numerous self-help books and doing exercises. I attended seminars, watched videos and basically tried anything to further my confidence. The more I worked on myself, in the same way that you are doing now by reading this book, the further I moved toward conscious competence.

Conscious Competence

Conscious competence is where you can apply a skill and yet you have to consciously think about applying the skill. The skill is not yet a habit for you. The vast majority of readers at this point in the book are probably consciously unstoppably confident. You know how to be confident, and now it's a matter of developing this into a habit. The twenty-one-day unstoppable confidence challenge does this. It forces you to deliberately practice your confidence for twenty-one consecutive days until you reach the skill level of unconscious competence.

Unconscious Competence

The fourth level of skill development is titled unconscious competence. This is the ultimate stage of any skill. *Unconscious competence* is when a skill has been ingrained as a habit. You no longer have to spend your time thinking about applying the skill.

People who are masters at what they do function at the level of unconscious competence. If someone were to inquire about how specifically they perform at such a high level, they may not be able to verbally describe what they do. The reason for this is because they are no longer conscious of what they do in order to perform such great feats.

Dedicate yourself to the good you deserve and desire for yourself.
Give yourself peace of mind. You deserve to be happy.
You deserve delight.
- Mark Victor Hansen

speaking the language of confidence

By changing your language you change your life.
— Kent Sayre

The Vocabulary Of Confidence

If you were to listen to others and yourself, you will notice that those people who are confident use a certain vocabulary and those lacking in confidence use an entirely different vocabulary. Most people use language unconsciously, which means they don't give it a lot of purposeful thought. As such, these habitual language patterns reflect a person's thinking, be it confident thinking or the lack thereof. Not only does language reflect a person's thinking, it also reinforces a person's thinking. When you change your language, you will reinforce new ways of thinking and begin to see a new perspective. As you do this, more options will become available to you while you naturally find yourself more confident. The key here is to integrate the following information into your everyday vocabulary. When this occurs, you'll not only change your thinking, you'll change your life!

So, what are these words? First of all, there are two sets of words. There's a set of words that you need to integrate into your vocabulary in order for you to be the most confident person that you possibly can. And there is a set of words that you need to absolutely eliminate from your vocabulary in order to help you get where you're going. Let's get down to it.

The Confidence Killers

First, we'll tackle the set of words to eliminate and completely remove from ✓ our vocabulary. If you catch yourself using these words, say, "Hey, wait a minute.

That was symptomatic of my old, shy self. And I'm no longer shy. I'm behaving confidently and, therefore, I have confidence. I'm going to use a different word." Don't beat yourself up over it. Just acknowledge that you use the word, eliminate it from your vocabulary next time, and go forth.

Try

The first word is "try." Have you ever heard someone try to do something? There's a difference between *trying* to do something and *doing* something.

Quite simply, trying is lying.

As you remember that, you can eliminate "try" from your vocabulary. Just like in *Star Wars*, when Yoda said, "There is no try, only do." Yoda was right on the money. There is no try. If you talk to someone and you say, "Hey, would you do this favor for me?" and they say, "I'll try," you can count on them not doing it. Because otherwise, they'd say, "Yeah, I'll do it."

Similarly, avoid using "try" in your own vocabulary. Instead, use the word "do." I will do it. I will perform this. I will do this favor for you. I will call you back. I will complete this task. Eliminate the word "try." Don't try to eliminate the word "try," do it. Eliminate the word "try."

The Shy Sentence: I'll try to do the laundry tomorrow.

The Confident Sentence: I will do the laundry tomorrow.

Hope

Another word that is not a word of confident people is "hope." Now, hope is nice and hope is surely better than nothing. However, "hope" presupposes a lack of action. Like, "I hope things get better. I hope my situation resolves itself."

Contrast this with "I'm going to take action and I'm going to make it happen." "I'm going to make my situation better." This is a subtle yet powerful difference between a reactive mindset. Hoping for something to happen is being reactive, whereas you are proactive when you take action and expect success.

Eliminate the notion "I hope that this could happen." Think, if you're using the word hope, stop yourself and say, "Now, what specific action could I take in order to make that happen or to maximize the likelihood of that happening?"

The Shy Sentence: I hope I can take a trip to Hawaii someday.

The Confident Sentence: I am making plans to take a trip to Hawaii next month.

But

"But" negates everything in the sentence that precedes it. An example is, "I want to go to a movie but I have a lot to do." In this example, it sounds as if the person will not be going to the movie. When someone hears the word "but," they immediately know that what was previously said should be disregarded. An example that is similar yet semantically different is, "I have a lot to do but I want to go to a movie." In this example, it sounds as if the person will be going to the movie. "But" always negates, so be aware of how you're using it if you do use it.

If you want to communicate the same thing without using the word "but," ✓ substitute these words: "and yet." So, suppose you need to turn down an invitation to an engagement. You could say, "Well, I'd like to do that and yet right now I still have something going on that prevents me from going."

The Shy Sentence: I want to go but I have something else going on.

The Confident Sentence: I want to go and yet I have something else going on.

The Three "oods": Would, Could, And Should   ✓

All right — would, could and should. The three "oods" that are no good. As we go through each "ood" we'll discover how their use in some places decreases confidence, and we'll learn how to replace them with words that will propel you even further to success.

Would

Would makes something conditional. It's not confident. It's not absolute. When I was discussing the notion that I was writing a book, some people were like, "Yeah, I would write a book too, if," then they'd give some reason that in their minds showed what's stopping them from going ahead and writing their own book. Or, "I would go meet that stranger and introduce myself." Well, "would" is conditional and presupposes there's something or some condition that's stopping you. So it's pointless to use the word "would." Eliminate that word from your vocabulary.

The Shy Sentence: I would talk to that stranger now if only…

The Confident Sentence: I will talk to that stranger now.

Could

"Could" is the next "ood" that we will eliminate. So if someone says, "I could go meet that person," then my question is, "What's stopping you?" Using what's known as the conditional tense of the word could implies that there is a condition attached to your action. Like, "I could go meet that person. I could go market my business to ten new people and expand it. I could make some calls on the phone and sell some more products. I could go give some strangers some compliments and smile at them and make them feel wonderful." "Could" presupposes that there's some condition that's stopping you. It's unnecessary. Eliminate it from your vocabulary. Preferably, use phrases like "I can," "I will," "I do."

The Shy Sentence: I could try making a speech in front of my peers.

The Confident Sentence: I can make a speech in front of my peers.

Should

"Should" is the worst of the "oods.""Should" implies that there's some sort of expectations projected onto you and that you lack a choice in how you want to behave. Think of the sentence, "I should be doing this right now." Well, you should be doing this according to whom? Ask yourself that, according to whom? Whose expectations? It's all about your own expectations, your own internal frame of reference. After all, you're running your brain, you're leading your own life. You're a unique, divine individual in charge of what you're doing. So, saying "should" is like keeping yourself hostage by limiting your choices. If you have a preconceived notion that you should do something all the time in a certain circumstance, then you're not going to investigate other options because you're just going to do what you "should do." And that's a limiting perspective because whenever you have fewer choices, you're less empowered and have less control over your life. Not good.

The Shy Sentence: It's late, and I should get home now.

The Confident Sentence: It's late, and I choose to go home now.

Attempt

All right, let me talk to you about the next word, which is "attempt." This word is similar to "try." When people say, "Hey, Kent. What are you going to do next?" I say, "I'm going to do this, I'm going to do this, and I'm going to do this." So, in the same way, the difference between doing something and attempting something is vast.

Think of a basketball player. She will tell you how many freethrows she's made and how many freethrows she has attempted. She understands the difference, and while it's a subtle nuance in wording, when you change your language you'll change your perspective in life and thus become more empowered. So again, consider your goals: you're going to go for them and you're going to achieve them. You *are* going to do this. You're not going to "attempt" to do this or that, you're going to go for it and you're going to do it. If you catch yourself using the word "attempt," that's fine. Simply switch your language and repeat the same phrase with the words, "I'm going to do this." Instead of saying, "I'm going to attempt this goal," say "I'm going to go after this goal, I'm going to achieve this goal, I'm going to accomplish this goal, I'm going to make this happen." When you speak the language of confidence, your life will become easier as you passionately pursue your goals. Speaking the language of confidence empowers you and reaffirms to yourself that you will achieve whatever you set to do.

The Shy Sentence: I'm going to attempt to water ski this afternoon at the lake.

The Confident Sentence: I'm going to water ski this afternoon at the lake.

Wish

The final word for you to eliminate to complete the first phase of building your vocabulary of confidence is "wish." Have you ever heard of wishful thinking? That's exactly that. Think of the associations the word "wish" creates in you: throwing a penny into some magic fountain and hoping that your wish will come true. And we already talked about what hope is. So just by wishing, it's as if you're not willing to take action and will it to happen, to do whatever it takes to accomplish what it is you want so you can lead the life of your dreams. So eliminate the word "wish" from your vocabulary.

The Shy Sentence: I wish that I'd win a million dollars.

The Confident Sentence: I want a million dollars and I'm taking specific, repeated, massive action to work my plan and get that million dollars.

The Confidence Builders

Now that we have talked about the words that we are eliminating from our vocabulary, let's discuss the words which, when you use them constantly and integrate them into your daily thoughts and speech, will skyrocket your confidence. The underlying principle is *definition of purpose*: words that show ✓ confidence, words that show that you know what you want.

Here are the words to add to your vocabulary for enhanced confidence:

- Absolutely
- Positively
- Without a doubt
- Certainly
- Obviously
- Naturally
- Definitely
- Assuredly
- Of course
- Undoubtedly
- Guaranteed
- Sure

What do all of these words do? They communicate a congruent message that "this is how it is and I'm confident of it and there's absolutely no doubt in my mind that this is the way it is."

Now, as you begin to use these words in your language, you will find the same thing. Notice how people respond as well, because they will respond differently to you. If someone asks, "What do you want to do?" there are a number of responses.

Here are two examples:

The Undecided Sentences: I don't know. I don't care. It doesn't matter to me.

The Confident Sentences: I absolutely want to see a movie tonight.

As you read them, you'll automatically notice the difference between someone who is confident and wants to do something and someone who may want to do something yet is too shy to say what.

Unstoppable Confidence – A Definition

As we have discovered in previous chapters, confidence is not a thing. Confidence is a process. As such, some may still think of confidence as something that is black or white, something that you either have or do not, but that's obviously not the case. People have varying levels of confidence in different contexts: they may be totally confident in their job, but not so sure of themselves while mingling with strangers. When you reach the state of **unstoppable confidence**, you will have ultimate belief in yourself. You will know that *you can do anything* you choose to do. Your confidence will be in yourself as a person, and cut across all contexts.

When you are unstoppably confident, you really do have the "go for it" attitude. When you are unstoppably confident, you never ask yourself, "Well, what if this goes wrong, what if that goes wrong? Is this even possible?" You flush all of that from your mind and instead begin to ask yourself, "How easily and naturally will I apply this? What will it take for me to go after this?" This way you're directing your unconscious mind that, "Hey, it's a given. It will happen. It's just a matter of what it will take."

When I began asking myself these questions, my real estate investing business really soared. I noticed a dramatic increase in my productivity and confidence level. This was because I was no longer asking myself, "Is this possible?" Instead, I would ask, "*What's it going to take?*"

Any question that you ask yourself, your mind will answer. For example, if you say, "Why am I so shy?" Then your mind, being the obedient answer-generating machine it is, is going to come up with the answers and say, "Well you're shy because a, b, and c."

Your unconscious mind will simply answer the questions you ask it, so stop asking the wrong questions start asking the right ones. Ask questions that will propel you to find empowering answers. So, ask yourself, "What's it going to take for you to do this? How much fun can you have if you accomplish what you want? How easily and naturally are you going to use all these skills in your life?"

Realize that the more you use these techniques, the faster and further you're going to accelerate on the confidence continuum, to the point where you're unstoppably confident. You'll look back and realize how far you've come and you'll naturally feel good knowing that you've gone so far, and that's just the beginning. Because life is about the journey, not just the end destination. We can't just get hung up on the ends or the result; life is about the journey, so let's enjoy it. Confidence is the same way. It is really quite enjoyable to experience the thrill of stepping outside your comfort zone and pushing yourself to do things you've never done before.

Why Confidence Matters

Let me talk a little bit now about why else confidence matters. We discussed this a little bit earlier. Without confidence, all your dreams would be stuck. You won't know that you have all the resources you need, that *you can achieve your dreams*. Also, we are naturally drawn to confident people. Imagine what it would be like to have people coming up just wanting to meet you simply because you are so confident; you automatically make an impression in their mind as being somebody different. Imagine how it feels to exude an attractive energy, one that radiates out and attracts people to you. People like people √ who are sure of themselves.

Being confident will immediately turbo charge your success in your business and your relationships because you come across as more credible. If someone asks you a question, you will look them straight in the eye, have confident physiology, and answer in an authoritative tone. Knowing absolutely that you believe in yourself, you give the plain answer and know you are correct. Then, you're going to come across as credible.

It took a few blown real estate deals for me to learn this lesson the hard way. I absolutely knew my stuff; I could easily get the job done. I knew it, yet I wasn't conveying it, so I had to shift on the unstoppable confidence because when I have the unstoppable confidence, I can definitely feel the difference in people. They trust me, they know I'm going to get the job done and I do, too. Part of being confident is when you're confident and communicating that to others, you're communicating that to yourself as well. That's just going to cause you to believe in yourself more, which will engender even more confidence.

Again, let me emphasize that confidence causes your dreams to come true. √ Right now, as I write this book, I am actually dictating it into an audiocassette recorder on a beautiful Thursday afternoon. I hear geese quacking in the background, everything is a gorgeous green right now in Oregon, there's a beautiful blue sky reflecting off a lovely pond. It's a puffy clouds kind of day, where you just want to relax and enjoy yourself, and because of using these techniques, I am able to be out here Rollerblading with my headphones on, listening to some of my favorite music, feeling absolutely wonderful, and this is my definition of enjoying myself.

Confidence gave me the ability to leave my job and start my own businesses. Confidence is what I needed to follow my dreams and I'm sure that as you read this, you can find your own reasons why it's important for you to go out and find your own dreams. And as you think about what your ideal bliss is, you can think about what it looks like, what it sounds like, what do you do on that day? Who are you with? How much fun are you having? How much are you enjoying yourself? What time do you get up? What time do you go to sleep? Do you take a nap because you can? How do you spend your time?

When you use these techniques and focus on your dreams, no matter what those dreams are, you'll develop the unstoppable confidence to go after your dreams and make them a reality. By keeping your vision in your mind, imagining it vividly and regularly, you automatically teach your unconscious mind to lead you to that day. And won't that day be wonderful?

There is a phrase that I really love: Nothing ventured, nothing gained.

Unfortunately, most people subscribe to the flipside, which is, "Nothing ventured, nothing lost." They don't take actions to get what they truly want, because if for some reason they don't make it, they won't have lost anything. They're thinking about all the risks, while you and I, we're focusing on all the rewards of going for what we want, aren't we?

So ultimately, and I mean ultimately, where does confidence come from?

You gain confidence from action. Confidence comes from doing.

If you know that you've done something one hundred times before and you have perfected it, you've gotten it down, you are just awesome at it — there's no substitute for that. It's much easier to approach the situation and do it.

"Hey, you are unstoppable. You're going to do this again and you're going to do it *great*."

This is the *ultimate* confidence.

On your journey toward unstoppable confidence, you will pass through three main stages. The first stage is at the *behavioral level*. By using the attitudes and techniques demonstrated in this book, you will behave as a confident person. Others will begin to treat you as if you were a confident person based upon your behavior. As you do this, it may seem at first unnatural and outside your comfort zone. That is good, because it means you are growing as a person and evolving on your journey.

The next stage on your journey to unstoppable confidence is at the *belief* ✓ *level*. By acting confidently, you will naturally develop the belief that you have confidence. At this time, you may have really powerful confidence in certain contexts. In the same way, you might experience other areas in your life where you need to still have more confidence. This stage of confidence is more powerful than the behavioral level since you believe you have the confidence as opposed to simply going through the motions of behaving confidently.

The third stage of confidence, which you will reach after you pass through the ✓ other two stages, is the *identity level* of confidence. This level epitomizes unstoppable confidence and means that you not only behave confidently and believe you have confidence, confidence is now a part of who you are. It's integrated into you as a person as part of your identity. This confidence runs through you like your blood travels through your body as your belief in yourself in doing anything you want is unwavering and completely concrete. People may question where you get such unstoppable confidence. Since it will be such a part of you and at such an unconscious level, you may not even know how you do it anymore because it's your natural state of being. This is the ultimate in unstoppable confidence.

Instead of having confident behavior, what if you were to be a confident person? The kind of person that simply *is* epitomizes and embodies what confidence really is. How would that be for you? And if you're not a totally confident person yet, how would that be different from how you are now?

Before you make this happen, you'll go through several steps on your journey to unstoppable confidence. There's also a confidence at the level of belief. This level means that you believe you're confident. You think so, you think you're confident. You're pretty sure. You say, "I am confident." But the ideal is to get to a point where you are so absolutely confident that it's a given. You don't need to think about it anymore. You are confident. You just are confident. It's your way of being. So, if you think about your beliefs, some of them, you're not even aware of them since they're just a given. It's just natural. If you've integrated your occupation into your identity, like you're a salesperson or you're a doctor, or you're a nurse, or you're an attorney or whatever. That's just a given. It's not a belief that you have. It's just your way of being. You know no differently.

We can do the same with confidence. While you are reading this now, just take a moment to consider how you think of yourself in relation to confidence. Whether you've considered yourself a shy person in the past, or you now realize that you are a confident person, understand that these are beliefs about yourself, beliefs about who you are. At first you may have had the old way of being; before you picked up this book you didn't know of any other way of being, of how truly resourceful and powerful you can be.

I know that for many of you, you thought of yourself as a shy person, someone who may not really speak up or make new friends easily, or you haven't even thought about how you can influence people at deep levels. When you think about your life, you can begin to realize just how you've experienced certain events, things that you did in your past, which led you to think that you were that way. You labeled yourself as shy, you generalized it, and built it as part of your identity.

As you realize this now and get an even better idea of how that worked, you can also understand how amazing it is. It shows how you can learn from memories and experiences, how you can easily and rapidly learn to do things and make them a part of your being.

How To Easily Motivate Yourself

Let's talk about how to use language to motivate yourself to do what you want. You can take any task or action that you don't particularly care about, and crank up your motivation so that you just have to do it.

Conversely, if there is something you are already motivated to do but you realize that it would be better if you didn't do it, you can use this technique to turn it into something you don't care about one way or another.

This goes back to our use of language and how it shapes our model of the world. With this technique, we will focus in on an aspect of language called *modal operators*. When you listen to someone's language, and especially their use of modal operators, you'll hear so much about how they move through the world, how they motivate themselves.

So what are modal operators? They are words or phrases like "must," "have to," "need to," "will," "can," "should," "would," etc. For our purposes, they fit into three categories: necessity, possibility and impossibility.

Modal operators of necessity indicate that something is necessary and that something needs to be done. They are words or phrases like:

- Have to
- Need to
- Must
- It's mandatory
- It's required

As such, using them in the right places in our language is excellent for motivation:

- "I *have to* take a break."
- "You *need to* go do some training."
- "We *must* work on this project now."
- "It's *necessary* to do your confidence exercises regularly and make them a part of you."

At the same time, modal operators of possibility open up possibilities to us. These words include:

- Can
- Could
- Might
- Possibly
- Maybe

When we use them in our language, they imply choice:

- "We have so many options we *can* pursue."
- "I *could* make it at 9:30 p.m. sharp. Easy."
- "Perhaps we *might* consider the new developments?"

Then we have modal operators of impossibility, words that imply that we simply cannot do something. '*Cannot*' is just one of those words:

- Cannot, can't
- Will not, won't
- Must not, mustn't

Notice how modal operators of impossibility close off options that may have been available to us:

- "I'll *never* go back to that old way of being."
- "You *must not* neglect to follow these instructions carefully."
- "I *can't* go a day without doing my unstoppable confidence exercises!"

So how do we use the knowledge of these things called modal operators to crank up your motivation? We do this by chaining them together — I want you to follow along in this example.

We will begin by saying a set of phrases, and each of them will differ in just a few subtle but powerful ways. Now, for the purpose of this exercise, for you to fully experience the impact of this technique, I want you to say each of these phrases out loud, congruently, confidently and powerfully. Take on a confident physiology; sit up straight, and say these phrases with an authoritative tone of voice.

We will begin by thinking for a moment about taking tomorrow off, or if it's a weekend as you read this now, taking off the upcoming Monday. Notice what it's like, notice how you feel as you think about this now. Notice how you represent the idea inside your mind. You motivation, your beliefs about whether or not you can do this, and every other associated thing will be influenced by how you say this to yourself.

As an exercise to help you understand how readily these seemingly simple words affect our motivation, we will take that notion through the spectrum of modal operators. Now I want you to say to yourself, "I can't take tomorrow off," and notice how you feel about taking the day off tomorrow.

Now say, "I couldn't take tomorrow off." Notice how using a modal operator of impossibility closes off that option.

Say the following sentence: "I can't take tomorrow off." *Can't* is a modal operator of impossibility in the present tense.

As you fully assume confident physiology, say aloud, "I couldn't take tomorrow off." While you do this, notice how that feels to you internally. Each time we exchange one of these modal operators for the other, the feeling will change.

Next, say aloud, "I could take tomorrow off." Using the word "could" will alter your experience as you find a different feeling within you by saying it. You might compare and contrast the differences between all of these sentences and think about how one word can so drastically alter the meaning and feeling of the sentence. "Could" shifts your thinking from that of impossibility into thinking that something is possible with conditions attached. To paraphrase the sentence, you could take tomorrow off if some condition were met. The part "if some condition were met" is implied through the usage of the word "could."

After the word "could," say the same sentence by replacing "could" with "can." "I can take the day off tomorrow." Your thinking has been shifted from a possibility to taking tomorrow off if some condition were to be met to a very real possibility in your mind that you in fact can right now as it stands take tomorrow off, if you choose.

To amplify the possibility of your taking tomorrow off, make the next replaced word in the sentence "may." Say to yourself out loud, "I may take tomorrow off." "May" presupposes that you may or may not take the next day off. "May" supersedes the ability that you can do something and, furthermore, suggests that you are considering whether or not to do it.

And notice your own motivation and contrast this to all the previous statements. Next, say, "I might take the day off tomorrow." When you think about how you might take the day off tomorrow, all of a sudden we've come from absolute impossibility to taking the day off to you're seriously considering taking the day off! You might take the day off tomorrow.

Next, use the next modal operator. "I should take the day off tomorrow." And hear this in the same voice that you tell yourself the things you should do. That voice that guides you in your daily life, that tells you what you should be doing at that proper time. "I *should* take the day off tomorrow."

Next, say to yourself, out loud of course, "I *shall* take the day off tomorrow." This has gone from conditional to should to shall. You're finally making your commitment to yourself to take the day off tomorrow because you deserve it after all, don't you?

Next, tell yourself, "I have to take the day off tomorrow." Really say, "I *have* to take the day off tomorrow!" as if you have to take the day off tomorrow. And notice how much more powerful that becomes. When you say, "I *have* to take the day off tomorrow!" you can feel it through every part of you. When you have to do something, you have to do it and then it'll be done.

Next, say, "I *need* to take the day off tomorrow." I need to. Taking a day off has gone from being a requirement to a *need*. A fundamental need. "I have to take the day off tomorrow! I *need* to take the day off tomorrow." This is the modal operator of the necessity working very powerfully here. And notice how your motivation increases that much more.

Finally, the modal operator that we've all been waiting for: "I *will* take the day off tomorrow." Say it congruently, authoritatively and powerfully. And notice how much, how committed you are to taking the day off tomorrow. As you look back on this exercise, you can find your motivation change because you've changed each word on the continuum of motivation. You've come from a place where it was absolutely impossible to take the day off tomorrow to your being committed to taking the day off. Simply by changing the words in our language.

Now, this is an example to demonstrate the power of these words, yet people are using these words all day long, all the time, to either limit themselves (modal operators of impossibility) or to motivate themselves (modal operators of necessity) or to empower themselves with more options (modal operators of possibility).

Adding More Choices To Your Life

Pay attention to how people use their language. As we have learned, language indicates how we view the world and it can be either empowering us or limiting us by what we say to ourselves and others. Some people unknowingly use their language to try to pass their limits on to you. Anytime someone offers you only one choice or another, be aware. Ask yourself if there are any other choices not mentioned. Is there anything stopping you from choosing both choices? The more options you have, the more empowered you are, which means you will have a greater chance of success in whatever you do. That alone is why we pay such close attention to our language to find the best choices available for us.

Salespeople are taught to intentionally use their language to limit our apparent choices. For example, let's suppose you've found a certain model of automobile you like. They might say something to the effect of, "Now that you've decided on this automobile, would you like to pay with all cash or do you want to finance it?" This question automatically assumes that you are going to purchase the car with the only remaining detail being how specifically you want to pay for it. Even if you did want to purchase the car, there may be another option that hasn't been mentioned due to the salesperson's limiting statement. What if there were a hybrid part-cash, part-financing option to purchasing the car? That is not reflected in the salesperson's statement.

Here are some questions to generate more options when you are presented with only a few:

- What's stopping us from doing both [all] the options?
- What if we were to do both [all] the options?
- What other options haven't we examined yet?
- Are these our only options?

Everything you want is out there waiting for you to ask.
Everything you want also wants you. But you have to take action to get it.

— Jack Canfield

the nine factors of unstoppable confidence

Courage is the first of human qualities because it is
the quality which guarantees all others.

— Winston Churchill

Confidence Is Experience

There are certain beliefs that are more empowering than others when doing
something for the first time. Believing the following will allow you to achieve
greater results more quickly.

When Doing Something For The First Time, Believe This: ✓

- The first time I do this is the hardest. ✓

- Each and every time I do this, it gets easier. ✓

- When I succeed, I will ask myself what I did well so I can ✓
improve even more.

- If I don't get my outcome, I'll learn from my mistakes and do ✓
things differently next time.

It does get easier. Hold that in mind as you overcome difficult tasks and minimize any adversity in doing something you have not done before.

In this book, I've given you many generalizations about confidence. Now
define what confidence means to you specifically. What will you see, hear, and
feel when you experience confidence? The reason it's important to know is
so that when you achieve the level of confidence you desire, you will know
that you have arrived.

With ultimate confidence in yourself, other people will begin to believe in
you. This will cause your belief in yourself to increase as the others count on

you. You will have the confidence to risk stepping outside your comfort zone. Consequently, you will discover yourself achieving things that were previously impossible. This in turn gives you more confidence, and others believe in you even further. This is the basis for the confidence success cycle. Your confidence and success increase cyclically as you continue to push the limits and achieve like you never have before.

Do what others believe is impossible. Remember that if they say it's impossible, they really only mean it's impossible FOR THEM.

Whether you like it or not, people will have opinions. Naturally, they are going to have opinions about you and your work. The key is to avoid letting their opinions affect you negatively. Personally, I live by the saying "What you think of me is none of my business." No one has ever really been successful by trying to please everyone all at once. The universe does not work like that. If someone says that something cannot be done or that it is impossible, realize that they are speaking **for themselves only**. If you hear people uttering those disempowering phrases, disregard them. They are not messages for you. They are chanting limiting, reinforcing mantras. Append the words "**for them**" whenever someone exposes their limiting beliefs to you.

What Things Really Mean

In the course of this book, I've introduced you to a lot of new concepts, some you've accepted, and others you've had to think about before they really made sense to you. I'll continue to give you new concepts and ideas, some of which may challenge your old way of thinking. Now I am going to introduce something that you may not believe at first, but as you think about it carefully you'll realize how pervasively this works in your life. Are you ready?

Meaning does not exist as an objective reality. Meaning is a purely subjective phenomenon.

How you think about something is entirely up to you. You can put a positive or negative frame of mind onto whatever experience you have in life. Since you always have a choice to either laugh or cry in life based upon your experience, do whatever you prefer. I prefer laughing, so I find myself doing that often.

A friend of mine was sitting in a park and told me this story. As he was sitting on a bench in a park, two drunks came by, one after the other. The first drunk came stumbling by and it was easy to see he was drunk. As he stumbled on by in a drunken stupor, he tripped over his own feet and fell face-first into the bushes next to the sidewalk. Dusting himself off, he quickly got up and glanced around to see if anyone was watching. Unfortunately for him, my friend was watching the entire episode. Noticing this, the drunk turned several shades of red before hurrying away as fast as he could.

Later on that same night, with my friend sitting at the same bench, another drunk came walking along the same path. At the same place in the sidewalk the drunk tripped and fell flat on his back. His spontaneous reaction was to let loose with a full belly laugh. He laughed so hard he began crying. He acted as if the slip was the funniest experience ever and it seemed he could not stop himself from laughing. By the time the drunk's laughter had died down, my friend was staring at him. Nonchalantly, the drunk picks himself up, smiles and acknowledges my friend, and happily darts off into the night.

The meaning of an experience, event, or interaction can widely vary between two people because it's their choice of what they make of it. If someone offers you an insult, remember that it's only their opinion. By adopting that useful belief, you can move through the world more resourcefully. Contrast this to how some people take insults personally and waste their valuable time and energy being bothered by it. You are a meaning-maker, and if you are giving something a less-than-useful meaning, stop yourself and give it a new meaning. Do this because you can.

In my own life, I had a business project that went sour. For a while, I spent my time being bitter and frustrated while being stuck in a victim mentality. Finally, I stopped that and started to ask myself questions like, *"What can I learn from this? What does this event really mean?"* When I asked myself these questions, I immediately shifted into a more useful mentality. What was a sore point became an opportunity for me to have the adversity mean that it's a challenge for me to rise above and conquer in order to achieve my outcome. As one thinks, so it shall be. And that is exactly what happened. Had I latched onto that victim mentality and refused to let it go, I never would have completed my business project. Any time you choose, you can change your state and make a new meaning for anything.

Confident Decision Making

People who have unstoppable confidence make decisions decisively and rapidly, and once a decision is made, they are committed to it. They rarely change their minds. They never waver because they know what they want. The main thing is knowing what you want beforehand, so when an opportunity presents itself to you or a problem presents itself to you, you can go inside yourself and find out, "Hey, is this congruent with what I want? Is this congruent with what I am after? Is this congruent with your personal policies? Is this congruent with my integrity?" Asking yourself all of these questions allows you to size up the decision you are making, so you can come back with a decisive, confident answer.

When someone commits themselves to their destiny, they go for it full tilt and consequently get their goals. The master motivational speaker, Anthony Robbins, says, "Success is cutting off all of your options for failure." As you realize what specifically you want out of life and decide that you're willing to pay the price to achieve it, commit yourself to cutting off all options of anything less than achieving your goal.

∨ Life is what you make it, so experience life on your own terms. Define the terms of your life and operate from them. Ask yourself, "What are my rules for this game of life? What will I accept for myself? What is unacceptable to me?"

∨∨ Life will pay any price you ask of it. The more you ask of life, the more you are willing to give, the more you'll get back in return. By the same token, the less you ask, the less you'll get. People with unstoppable confidence ask for all of their dreams to come true. They do this by setting their goals, getting the tools to make them happen, then they take committed, massive, immediate, repeated action to make them real. Others ask for only some of their dreams to come true and thus set fewer goals, take less action in a less-committed manner, and consequently get fewer results. This choice is entirely up to you and how you choose to live your life.

Let me go through the step process of confident decision-making. Prior to undertaking anything, have your goals set up, know what you want; have your personal policies, your integrity, know who you are, what you stand for, and what is acceptable and unacceptable. This will help you in the confident decision-making process.

So before anything else, you need to take an inventory of yourself. Get to know yourself, who you are, what you stand for, where you are going, and how you are going to get there. When you know this, everything else becomes very simple.

Now, if you have a question, a problem, or an opportunity that comes to you, you need to size up the situation from all angles in order to be a confident decision maker. Look at it from your position. Look at it from the other side.

Look at the position and how it will affect you throughout time. If you were to say yes to this decision and move forward with it, how would this impact your life? Imagine yourself a few months down the road, one year down the road, five years down the road, after having said yes to this decision. How is your life? Explore how the future may be if you said no. Now consider, how might your life be if you say no to this decision? A few weeks from now, a few months from now, a few years from now? And once you get that picture clearly in mind, decide if that's congruent with your goals. Let your goals be your road map.

Without any goals, people are like ships without rudders. They float along in the sea. So often I meet people and I say, "What do you want out of life? What are you looking to do?" And they say, "I want to be happy," or "I just want success," or "I just want to be rich." And I say, "Great, what does happiness specifically mean to you? What does success specifically mean to you? What does a lot of money specifically mean to you?" Too often, I get glazed over looks as people don't know the answer to those question.

People need to get very clear, to be very open and honest with themselves about what these words mean for them. For some people, being rich means making $100,000 a year. For others it might mean making five million dollars a year. And for others, it could be something different altogether. Everyone is an individual and unique. They need to define what they want and what specifically the meaning is of the following words; "happiness," "security", "freedom," "love," "success," "riches." After they have defined what these words mean, they will know how close they are to getting those. And in defining these words, they should think about what they will see, hear, feel, experience, think, and believe when they have those. That way, one knows with absolute certainty if they are experiencing it. Are you happy? You know if you have happiness defined. You will know you are successful when events around you fit the definition that **you** have decided upon. Confident people march to the beat of their own drummers. They don't care what society thinks. They don't care about other people projecting their expectations or their limits onto them. They are going after what they want, doing what they believe.

You will immediately know how to make a decision once you know what your ultimate goals and directions are in life. Simply knowing where you truly want to be in life simplifies your task so much because this knowledge becomes the yardstick by which you measure progress, and the compass you use to navigate to **your** success.

The Structure Of Empowerment

When you are unstoppably confident, there is a singular difference between you and the "normal" population. This difference is control. You have more control over your environment, over yourself, over your emotional state, over your thinking, over beliefs, and ultimately over your actions. That is quite simply the difference between people who are empowered and people who are not. People who are not empowered have excuses. They have all the reasons why it is impossible to be, do, or have something. Those who are unstoppable realize that everything they ever want to do is in their control. They are the masters of their own universe. And if they don't know how to do something, they realize that there's someone out there, a book, a seminar, or a course that will teach them how to do it.

I like to think of myself as a "reverse paranoid."

A reverse paranoid is: *A person who thinks that the universe is perfect and good and everybody on the planet wants to help them out and help them achieve their dreams.*

Now by the law of reciprocity, in order to fulfill my dreams, I'm going to help serve others. The universe works and rewards those who serve others. Therefore, the more we help others, the more we will be rewarded for our good deeds. The greater the energy you put forth coupled with the greater service you provide to others, the more results you will enjoy. When you ask yourself, "How can I be of service to others today?" you will experience a paradigm shift of great proportions.

Empowered people have more choices than disempowered people. Disempowered people do not allow themselves to find other choices that are available to them. Always contemplate the number of choices you have in any given situation and do your best to generate more options. Perhaps there is an option you have not thought of that would be ideal. All you need to do now to empower yourself is to think of it and then act on it. With greater empowerment comes a greater sense of freedom, because you have a freedom to choose from more options.

Disempowered people simply lack choices and are thus compelled to act upon their addictions not out of choice, but out of sheer necessity. Even if we were to consider psychopathic criminals, they appear as if they are "forced" to perform their evil deeds. In interviews, they often reveal how they went to great lengths to cover up what they did because they internally understood that it was wrong. Inevitably, the question as to why they perpetuated the violent acts if they truly understood the acts were immoral and wrong gets posed to them. They acknowledge that while they know it's wrong, they feel as if they have no other option and their criminal acts were their only choice. Again, this is simply their perception of reality of the criminal acts being their only choice.

I am not condoning or apologizing for criminal behavior, but rather pointing out the fact that people need to make better choices for themselves, and to do that they first need to become aware of those choices and realize their validity.

The more choices you have, the more empowered you are. The more empowered you are, the better the choices you will make because the quality of their choices is so much higher. If the only choice is to cater to this addiction and there is nothing else possible, then what are people going to do? They are obviously going to cater to the addiction.

The initial step to becoming more empowered is to eliminate the belief that "You have few choices" and replace that belief with "You have a lot of choices. You always have a freedom to choose. No matter what situation, even in times where there is an apparent lack of choice, there really is a choice." When you keep this belief as you go through life, you will be enriched as you have a sense of control over your life, which escapes most people.

Confidence Comes From Action

Confidence comes by finding out what specifically you want, making a plan ✓
to get that, and going for it! If you're doing well, ask yourself what you're doing
well and consequently make it even better. If you haven't yet been getting the
results you want, evaluate what you are doing wrong, adjust your behavior
based upon the feedback you're getting, and do things differently. As much as
I'd like to say that all you have to do is perform these mental techniques and
you'll have confidence, undisputed real confidence comes from doing. Now,
these mental techniques will help you out, guaranteed. Yet, if you stop and
think about the most confident people out there in our world, you'll find they
are confident because they have proven to themselves over and over again
that whatever they are confident at is because they have done it so many
times that they know from the deepest parts of their heart, mind, and soul
they are capable doers. The process of confidence takes two steps: Take
action and get confidence. It's not backward, like get all the confidence and
then take action. Taking action gains you the undisputed, real confidence
you desire and deserve.

Confidence And Goal-Orientation

The natural complement to unstoppable confidence is being goal oriented. ✓
Goal orientation and confidence make for a combination that will make all ✓
of your dreams come true. Have the long-term vision of what you want your
life to become. Set up your long-term goals so that when fully realized, you will ✓
find yourself living your dream lifestyle.

With your long-term vision defined, plan out your medium-range goals. Your
medium-range goals are the goals that are in-between your immediate
shortterm goals and your long-term vision. When you accomplish your
medium- term goals, you will know you are on the right track to achieving
your long-term goals.

Break down all of your medium-range goals into short-term goals. These
short-term goals can be goals you will accomplish in the next year. Then continue breaking down the goals until you have monthly goals and then weekly
goals and then specific actions you will take each and every day to move
you ultimately to your dream life. Set an outcome for everything you do and ✓
live life with purpose. You will be glad that you did.   ✓

The way one summits a mountain is to continue to put one foot after another toward the top. The way one runs a marathon is to put one foot after
another. It's essential to keep going. Never quit. Do it now. If I had to bet on
someone's success, I'd always pick someone who is dumb and persistent
rather than someone who is a genius yet gives up easily.

Outcomes vs. Goals

Outcomes and goals are similar yet differ in scope. Goals are typically of larger magnitude than outcomes. An outcome is whatever you want to get out of any activity or interaction. A goal is a dream with a deadline.

When I hang out with my friends, my outcome is to have a good time and to make them feel good. I don't have a goal when I'm hanging out with them. My goal is to sell a certain number of copies of this book within the next year. The magnitude of my goal and my outcome differ. While outcomes can be much smaller in scope, they are still very useful. By identifying what you want out of any activity or interaction, you will be much more likely to actually fulfill that outcome than if you did something without purpose. If I don't know what I want out of an interaction or activity, how would I know how to focus in and get it? How would I know how to evaluate my feedback and change my behavior to get my outcome if I don't have a preset outcome? I wouldn't!

After you decide on your outcome or goal, figure out what it's going to take to accomplish it. What kind of person will you have to be in order to make your dreams come true? Then commit to becoming that kind of person. You already have the confidence to do it or you're rapidly gaining the necessary confidence through practicing the methods in this book.

There is a simple three-step approach to living your dreams: *be, do* and *have*. The *be* means to be the person you were always meant to be as you reach as much of your potential as humanly possible. As you grow into being that person, *do* whatever it takes and make the activities happen, which promote your dream life. After you *do* all of that, you will *have* your ideal lifestyle. It's really as simple as that.

When you're starting out and figuring out who to become, choose what tools you deem necessary for your journey. Then go out and get those tools that you haven't acquired yet. These could be communication skills, confidence skills (this book), entrepreneurial skills, relationship skills, particular skills to your profession, etc.

Refrain from asking yourself questions like "Is it possible? Can I do this?" Why would you avoid asking those questions? Because you already know you can do it! Presuppose it as a given. You can accomplish whatever you set your mind to accomplish. With the possibility of your venture already firmly established, ask yourself, "What is it going to take to accomplish my venture?" This presupposes that the feasibility of your project is already entrenched as a definite yes in your mind and now the only thing to determine is how specifically you will carry out the project.

By asking yourself, "What's it going to take to do this?" you effectively squelch the negative internal voice. It's like you grab the voice and put it in the corner, wrapping up its mouth with duct tape as you admonish, "Hey you, negative internal voice, go stay over there in the corner. I'm going to get my outcome, so just be quiet now and forever onward. Got it!?!"

Understanding Your Patterns Of Motivation

Pleasure Or Pain?

Another key to being a go-getter is how you motivate yourself. Do you motivate yourself with pleasure or with pain? Do you think about all the excellence you want in your life or all the trouble you don't want in your life? You motivate yourself one of those ways and only you know that. Are you moving toward your goals and positive things or are you moving away from problems and negative things?

Both strategies can be effective in certain contexts. The strategy of avoiding pain and problems can be effective. For example, trial lawyers often using a pain avoidance strategy as preparation for their argument in order to construct strong cases for their clients. They seek to minimize any damage or trouble that the opposing attorneys may try to inflict by creating strong counter arguments. The strategy of seeking pleasure and getting excellence can be equally effective. In fact, a large majority of the most successful people who have close family relationships, who have massive success in their careers and businesses, and who make more money have motivation strategies drawing them toward more intimacy and communication, more and better service for their customers, and more efficiency in working intelligently to get their goals.

You may have already realized which motivation style you predominately utilize. In having unstoppable confidence, I encourage you to focus on having a positive motivation strategy that allows you to seek more pleasure and better things in your life. Doing this goes back to modeling people who are already successful. The most successful people have the positive motivation, and if we want their results, then naturally we can behave as they do to replicate these results.

To Whom Do You Listen?

Another difference between people who have unstoppable confidence and those who do not is their trust in their internal voice. Although people who have unstoppable confidence listen to others for feedback, they tend to rely more and place more weight on their own internal voice than the external voices of those around them. People who lack unstoppable confidence tend to listen to the external voices of those around them. This leads to a propensity for conformist thinking because people listening to and following everyone else will be like everyone else. People who are unstoppable have to rely on their own internal voices, or otherwise they would allow everyone else with "stinking thinking" to convince them that whatever goal they are seeking to accomplish cannot be done. Listening to your own internal voice means that you recognize what is valid and useful feedback and what is negative and destructive criticism. People who listen to their internal voice are said to have an <u>internal frame of reference</u>. People who follow the external voices of others are said to have an external frame of reference.

The way to discover for yourself your personal style, if you haven't already, is to ask yourself the following questions:

- If nobody told you what to do, would you know what to do?

- How do you know you've done a great job?

- Does someone else need to tell you or do you know internally?

- How do you know what you should be doing at any time?

Now, as you answer each of those questions honestly, you might notice a pattern emerging. Should your answers be inclined to be based on others' feedback, right now you have more of an external frame of reference. If your answers are inclined to be based on your own internal voice or your gut feeling, you have more of an internal frame of reference.

People may have different frames of reference in different contexts. Unstoppable people have internal frames of reference in areas that matter most: family, career, spirituality, business, finances, goals, etc. Frames of reference matter less in smaller contexts.

One such context is deciding whether to go watch a movie or not. This example demonstrates the stark difference in frames of reference. My friend and I used to attend movies together. She had a heavy external frame of reference when it came to deciding which movies to see and I had a heavy internal frame of reference. She would ask her friends or relatives and read critics' reviews of a movie before it came out. With my internal frame of reference, I would either see the preview of the upcoming movie myself or would read a synopsis of the movie. With these two polarized decision strategies as to which movies to visit, the results were somewhat amusing. If she suggested the movie and we both liked it, everything was fine. If I suggested the movie and we both like it, everything was fine. However, if she selected the movie and I disliked it, I would confess to her that when I saw the previews I thought it was going to be a stinker of a movie. She would counter with how her family, friends, and the critics raved about it. In the same way, if I chose a movie and she disliked it, she would in no uncertain terms inform me of how awful the critics thought it was and how all her friends tried to convince her not to see it. Had I not been aware of the difference between the external and internal frames of reference, this could have been a source of tension but fortunately awareness prevented that.

So along with all of the other goals that you are setting, I want you to set a goal for your confidence. I want you to set a specific, measurable, achievable, realistic goal for your confidence.

To make this even stronger, here's what I recommend. I've used this in the past for goals in all areas of my life and I always find it to be amazingly effective, to the point where I keep coming back to it over and over again.

Write out your goal, using all of the SMART criteria that we have discussed, and at the bottom, make a space for your signature, your name and the date. At the top of this sheet, call it a Goal Contract. Contracts are taken very seriously, particularly here in the United States. The legal definition of a contract is a meeting of minds, so as you write out this contract and sign it, think of it as a meeting of your conscious and your unconscious minds. This becomes a 'legally binding' document, a legal contract that you **must** execute because of its binding power.

The Value Of Negative Motivation

While having a strategy to move towards excellence can be beneficial in certain circumstances, you can also benefit by having a strategy that moves away from pain. Since we all move toward pleasure or away from pain, we are motivated to some degree in all contexts by one or the other or by both. Because I wanted to get this book done in a timely manner, I committed myself to not only moving toward the pleasure of having the book published and also committing myself to pay a monetary fine if I'm not on target and meeting my writing goals. In having the "away from pain" motivation, my efforts skyrocketed as I instantly became tremendously more productive. As you think about how I've applied this, you can begin to contemplate all the ways in which you can have "toward pleasure" and "away from pain" motivation methods implemented in your own life now.

When you set up your "away from pain" strategy, make it something more than slightly annoying if you were to not follow through and yet not catastrophic if for some unknown reason you do not achieve your outcome. Your strategies ought to be proportional to the magnitude of your goal you will accomplish. Here's an example to further your understanding. If you're on a diet and you have a piece of cake, you obviously won't punish yourself by fasting for the rest of the week. That would be ridiculous. You want your pleasure rewards and pain punishments commensurate with the goal. Continuing onward with the example, if you eat some chocolate cake while you're on a diet, you might figure out how many calories you ingested so the next time you work out, you will burn that many extra calories beyond your normal workout.

People become addicted to various things at all times. Gambling, drugs, and alcohol are a few of the many destructive addictions people have. People inherently have addictive mechanisms within them. The secret key is to aim our addictions in a positive direction. What would it be like to be addicted to healthy eating, to practicing and enhancing your spirituality, to doing something new and different each day, to chatting with strangers and being friendly, to promoting your business, to figuring out ways to be more productive at your job? How would life be different if you were addicted to those things? People practice their addictions very faithfully but they typically aim them in the wrong direction. What if you are addicted to becoming more organized and efficient in everything you do? What if you were addicted to spreading joy and ecstasy in your life and the lives of those people around you? How about if you were addicted to becoming more productive?

People who have unstoppable confidence have it because confidence is a habit of theirs. The difference that makes the difference in our lives is the quality and kinds of habits we have in our lives. Each of us have habits and addictions. Let's empower ourselves to have positive, life-affirming habits and addictions. Habits are tremendously powerful and a necessity in our lives. Without habits, we'd have to consciously do everything all the time. It simplifies life to have habits and to just do things. The problem occurs if we don't make ourselves aware of our damaging habits and change them.

There'd be so many decisions to make; we'd easily go on information overload, as if we're not there already. And we might go nuts. Habits simplify our lives because we don't have to think about what to do, we just do it. That's why it's critical to develop good habits. On your goal contract, make it one of your goals to develop the confidence habit. Make it another goal to notice yourself becoming more and more confident and evaluate your progress.

I strongly recommend you keep a confidence journal so you can chart your progress to see just how far you've come. By the time you are fully aware that you have unstoppable confidence, you'll be able to review your journal and you'll naturally be amazed to discover just how differently you think and how far you've come. By regularly reviewing your journal, you'll be able to immediately correct yourself so that you can have more confidence in the immediate future. In your journal, feel free to jot down notes on what specific techniques from this book you will utilize in the next interaction to cause you to be even more confident.

The Value Of Momentum

Momentum is very valuable in terms of increasing your confidence level. One of Newton's laws of physics states that an object at rest tends to stay at rest unless acted upon by an outside force. Similarly, an object in motion tends to stay in motion unless acted upon by an outside force. The same law applied to confidence states: for people stuck and at rest, it may be a bit difficult for them to begin increasing their confidence. However, after they overcome any initial resistance, they will accelerate the rate at which they gain confidence in themselves. For people who have unstoppable confidence, it's even easier for them to accelerate their confidence-gaining rate.

Stop for a moment and take a survey of how much momentum you have in your life. Are you in motion? Are you out there making it happen? Or are you going a little slower? Only you can honestly judge this for yourself. Do you need to crank it up a notch? No matter where you are at, you can increase your momentum. The best way to do this is by starting small. As you continue to do small things each and every day, you step closer and closer to your goals. The small things add up and pretty soon you will be leading the life of your dreams. After you're at the top of your mountain, having fulfilled all of your goals, you can look back at what you've done and marvel at how you took all those small actions each and every day and they added up to your massive success. These small actions to thrust you toward your goals can be any number of things. Some examples include: checking out a tape set from the library, purchasing some books on a relevant topic, or attending a seminar where you will learn what you need to empower yourself.

The way I became a full-time real estate investing entrepreneur was by subscribing to the aforementioned strategy. I learned a branch of real estate investing called Creative Real Estate Investing that requires neither money nor credit because when I started I had neither! What I did to allow myself to go full-time into the business was read a lot of books, attend a few seminars on real estate, make some offers on houses each week, and make calls to sellers after work every day. Every day you are either moving toward your goals or away from them. Personally, I want to always be moving further toward my goals with each passing day. Momentum is infinitely powerful and you can make it work for you or against you. Make it work for you.

The Power Of Commitment

Commitment is very powerful in enabling you to get your dreams. Many people say, "Don't burn your bridges." I'm just the opposite. I say, "Learn to burn and burn very well!" Find out what you want to do, commit yourself to it one hundred percent, and then burn away any options for failure. Ask yourself about all the excuses that might prevent you from accomplishing your goal. After you do that, go through and torch each bridge so that the only option is success because you've committed yourself to that result.

When I left my corporate job as an engineer in a major semiconductor company, I mentally, emotionally, and spiritually committed to living the lifestyle of my dreams by burning all of my bridges. All of my ties to the company and potential for getting a job back instantly vanished. Even if I went back begging for a job, no job would be available to me. Success becomes the *only* option. Just as I did, you can do the same with what you want. Decide what you want, commit to it, and systematically burn all bridges that might prevent you from getting exactly what you want.

Courage is resistance to fear, mastery of fear — not absence of fear.

— Mark Twain

beyond belief

If you develop the absolute sense of certainty
that powerful beliefs provide, then you can get yourself
to accomplish virtually anything, including those things
that other people are certain are impossible.

— Anthony Robbins

Your Current Beliefs Realized

Pause for a moment and consider everything around you. Everything you have and everything you lack is directly a result of a belief of yours. Similarly, all of your experiences you have completed and those experiences yet to be done are because of your beliefs. Beliefs are pervasive throughout all areas of our life and influence what we do and how we do what we do to an extraordinary degree. The quality of one's life depends upon the quality of the beliefs ✓ that one holds. The more useful and empowering the beliefs you hold, the ✓ more success you will attract into your life.

Beliefs are very influential to us in our lives. They have the ability to cause us to take action and fulfill our dreams or to keep us stuck. What makes the difference is the quality of the beliefs. By following a person's actions, you can deduce their beliefs. If someone has a successful and happy relationship, you can deduce they believe in commitment to their partner. If someone has well-raised kids, you can deduce that the parents believe in taking pride in being good parents. If someone is very fit and muscular, you might guess that person values health and fitness.

How Beliefs Are Formed

As we go through our lives, we have different sets of experiences. For each of these experiences, we make meaning out of them. If we have a consistent set of experiences, we generalize something and believe in it as if it were always true.

By creating generalizations in life, we save ourselves time and energy in doing things. We do things automatically and don't have to relearn how to perform certain tasks that include opening a door, driving a car, and riding a bicycle.

We acquire beliefs not only through our own experiences but also through learning from people who are authority figures in our lives. They pass on their beliefs to us. Usually, to young children these are parents and teachers. During this period, we didn't consciously filter what we wanted to believe or whether a belief was empowering to us. Since they were authority figures, we simply adopted their beliefs as if they were always true all the time. This is largely useful, yet sometimes those same well-meaning authority figures pass on less-than-useful beliefs.

We have many beliefs that have simply been passed onto us. Instead of consciously choosing our beliefs, we automatically adopt our parents', teachers' and other authority figures' beliefs. As adults, we can realize that there is a better way. That way is to adopt beliefs based on their utility to you. Does the belief serve you? If so, keep it. If the belief keeps you stuck, get rid of it and replace it with a more empowering belief.

You can learn from each and every person, and when you find they have empowering beliefs in a certain area, you can adopt those beliefs for yourself. Similarly, be sure to filter out any limiting beliefs that someone may try in vain to pass onto you.

Consistently identify your beliefs about different things in different contexts. Make it a habit to eliminate the useless ones. Make it a habit to even more powerfully believe in the empowering ones.

Sometimes people mislabel their feelings and create faulty beliefs. If someone gets excited before selling something and they mistakenly label it fear, they may create a belief that selling means it's time to get scared. The next time they go out to sell, it will be harder for them if they believe they are about to get scared. Pay close attention to how you label your emotions because that will determine whether you create useful or useless beliefs.

The Structure Of Beliefs

Beliefs are structured in two different ways. They are built out of meaning and causality. When you hear either "meaning" or "causality" language, you know someone is sharing their beliefs with you. I personally find it useful to listen for people's beliefs, and whenever they have a more empowering belief than one I currently hold, I replace my belief with theirs. Using the same idea, if they share a belief that I find less than useful to myself, I simply respect their belief and avoid adopting it as my own.

Meaning beliefs are structured in these forms: "X **means** Y" or "X **is** Y." Causality beliefs are structured in these forms: "X **causes** Y" or "X **because** of Y." You are listening to beliefs whenever you hear one of the following words: "means," "is," "causes," and "because." When you hear beliefs, realize that they are not necessarily true. Sometimes people forget that fact, and accidentally take on less- than-empowering beliefs for themselves. This is especially true for people listening to authorities, who forget to question what beliefs the authority is trying to promote.

Types of Beliefs:

Meaning Beliefs: *X means Y.*
                        X is Y.

Example: A hot stove means I shouldn't touch it.
                        A hot stove touched is painful.

Causal Beliefs: *X causes Y.*
                        Y because of X.

Example: If I touch a hot stove, it will cause
                        me to burn myself.

                        I'll burn myself because I touch a hot stove.

The Qualities Of Beliefs

Beliefs have certain mental qualities about them that allow them to be encoded as beliefs in your mind. Intuitively, this is obvious that there must be some way the mind differentiates between what is a strongly held belief and what is a weakly held belief. To put it another way, there has to be some way that your mind knows what you are absolutely sure of and what you are unsure of.

Each belief has certain visual, auditory, and feeling qualities associated it. By altering any of these qualities, we alter the belief. In consciously directing our minds, we can deliberately manipulate these qualities in order to keep only the most empowering beliefs that serve us.

Visual Qualities Of Experience

Movie stars are often adored to the point where they are mobbed by fans and are glamorized as larger-than-life. The reason for this is because they are literally presented as larger-than-life on huge movie screens in theaters. In the same way, when you think about certain things on your *mental* movie screen, things will seem very compelling. If you have something that you want to experience more of, you can increase the size of whatever it is you are picturing in your mind and notice how that feeling becomes more intense.

Another way to make a belief more intense is to make it brighter and closer. Just like sitting in the front row in the movie theater, you can do the same thing in the movie theater of your mind. The brighter and closer something is, the more intense the feeling you will experience.

The converse is similarly true. If you want to make something less powerful, you can make it small, dark, and far away. To lessen the intensity even further, you can make the picture of what you're thinking about black and white. It's why movies are no longer made in black and white. Color movies are more compelling and move, touch, and inspire people in a way black and white movies cannot. When you run your mind consciously, take everything good and make it big, bright, close, and colorful. Furthermore, take everything that is negative and push it away to make it small, dark, far away, and in black and white.

People often encode their experience to have their negative experiences big, bright, close, and colorful while having their positive experiences small, dark, distant, and black and white. Doing this means that people will have more of a negative disposition because the negative images are more compelling in their minds. Deliberately running your mind means you encode your experiences and beliefs in the most useful way to you.

Auditory Qualities Of Experience

Just like the visual qualities of experiences and beliefs affect the intensity, so too do the auditory qualities affect the intensity. Going back to my movie theater analogy, people have a more intense experience in the theater when the sound is loud, engulfing the people in stereo surround-sound that is crystal clear while the bass reverberates within their bodies. Contrast this with having a movie theater with low volume, mono-sound only in the front of the theater that sometimes has static to it. The latter kind of sound is much less compelling than the former kind of sound and consequently there is much less feeling associated with the latter kind of sound. Watching and listening to a movie in a theater with the weak sound is a completely different experience than watching and listening to a movie with the powerful sound.

We can deliberately alter our experience and the power of our beliefs by altering the sound qualities associated with it. By turning the volume up or down and changing the location of the sound, we can experience different feelings.

Feeling Qualities Of Experience

By altering the visual and auditory qualities of our beliefs and experiences, we change the feelings associated with them. If you want excellent feelings, you need to see and hear excellent things. Now that you understand how to deliberately change your past memories, current experiences, and beliefs, you can practice making your good memories even better, your past less-than-glorious memories more neutral, and very powerfully lock in your most empowering beliefs.

For a complete description of all the qualities that a person can change to alter their beliefs and experiences, please refer to Appendix A.

How To Change Your Beliefs ... For Good!

Right now I want you to use what you've just learned by offering you a simple way to change your beliefs, perhaps faster and more effectively than you ever dreamed possible. The first belief that we will change is any old thoughts or self-images you may have had about being shy, and we'll replace that with being confident and moving through the world in a whole new way. Avoid using this for just one belief, because you can use this for *any* belief that may have been holding you back. Use this method to change all beliefs that you find less than glorious and less than resourceful.

Read through the instructions a few times to familiarize yourself with what you are about to do, and you may also like to get a partner to help guide you through this, someone who is supportive of your transformation, perhaps someone who is on that same transformational journey. Your partner can read these instructions out to you, or you can simply take note of the instructions. Close your eyes and do this now.

You have certain mental pictures, sounds, and feelings that are associated with beliefs. What we're going to do is basically change the structure of the belief and thereby change the belief. By altering the structure of the belief, we alter how the mind encodes the belief. The mind encodes powerful beliefs differently from weakly held beliefs.

The overview of this process is to first find out how you doubt something. Then we'll bring you back to your normal, neutral state of being. Third, we'll discover how you believe in things strongly. We'll again bring you back to your normal, neutral state of being. Finally, we will change your beliefs. We will take your limiting belief and turn it into a doubt. By doubting your limiting belief, you free yourself from it. We will take your empowering belief and lock it into your mind as a strongly held belief.

Step One: Discover How You Doubt

The first thing to do is to close your eyes and think of something that you used to believe to be true but no longer do. For example, you might think about how as a child, you believed in Santa Claus but no longer do. As you think about that belief, become aware of everything you see associated with the belief. More importantly, since we are paying attention to the structure of the belief, look at the different visual qualities of the belief and make mental notes of them.

Regarding what you see and your belief that is no longer true but used to be:

- Is it flat or 3-D?
- Does it have a frame around it?
- What size is it?
- Is it clear or out of focus?
- How bright is it?
- Where is the location of the belief?

With your eyes still closed, tune in to the sounds that are associated with your belief that used to be true but no longer is. Listen closely and pay particular attention to the sound qualities as you answer the following questions:

Regarding what you hear and your belief that is no longer true but used to be:

- Do you hear a voice of doubt?
- Do you hear a voice of authority?
- Do you hear other sounds?
- How loud are the sounds you hear?
- What location do the sounds come from?

Step Two: Break State

Open your eyes, take a deep breath, and name three different things in the room. This will help you shift from a doubt state back to your neutral state. Even physically move to another place if you need to return to your neutral, normal state.

Step Three: Discover How You Believe

Think of something you know is absolutely true. Pick out something that you have no question about and believe one hundred percent that it is true. Something simple, like "The sun will rise tomorrow," or "I need to breathe air to live." We're going to elicit the same visual and sound qualities in this powerful belief that we just elicited for the doubting belief.

As you think about this absolutely true belief, become aware of everything you mentally see associated with the belief. More importantly, since we are paying attention to the structure of the belief, look at the different visual qualities of the belief and make mental notes of them.

Regarding what you see and your strongly held belief:

- Is it flat or 3-D?
- Does it have a frame around it?
- What size is it?
- Is it clear or out of focus?
- How bright is it?
- Where is the location of the belief?

With your eyes still closed, tune in to the sounds that are associated with your belief that is absolutely certain. Listen closely and pay particular attention to the sound qualities as you answer the following questions:

Regarding what you hear and your belief that is absolutely true:

- Do you hear a voice of doubt?
- Do you hear a voice of authority?
- Do you hear other sounds?
- How loud are the sounds you hear?
- What location do the sounds come from?

Step Four: Break State

When you're done making mental notes of all the qualities of what you see and hear, open your eyes. Take a deep breath and point out three different things in the room. This will help you shift from your strong belief state back to your neutral, normal state of being. Physically get up and move to another location if it helps you to return to your normal state.

Step Five: Change The Belief

Think of a limiting belief of yours. Since this is a book about confidence, think of a belief about your confidence or shyness or ability to do something. A good example is "I can't go up and meet strangers easily." This is a belief that limits many people, and their social and business lives would improve if they rid themselves of that belief.

Once you've selected your limiting belief regarding confidence or shyness, close your eyes and notice all the visual and audio qualities of that belief. This is the same thing we've done in steps one and three. After you've gotten the visual and audio qualities of that belief, begin to change each and every visual and audio quality of your limiting belief to match all of the visual and audio qualities of something that you used to believe but no longer do — an *old* belief. This recodes your limiting belief and transforms it into a something you no longer believe. When you have done this properly, you will find the limiting belief to be an *old* belief, something you *used* to believe but no longer do. Make sure that the visual and audio qualities of the limiting belief match those of the old belief as precisely as possible.

When you're done transforming that belief, open your eyes. Take a deep breath and point out three different things in the room. This will help you shift back to your neutral, normal state of being. Physically get up and move to another location if it helps you to return to your normal state.

Congratulations on removing that limiting belief. Since nature abhors a vacuum, we will place an empowering belief in your mind where the limiting belief used to reside. To do this, think about something with respect to your confidence that, when you believe it, your life will improve.

Now as you close your eyes, think of the belief that you want to believe fully. As you become aware of the visual and audio qualities of that belief, begin to change each and every quality of that belief to match precisely the visual and audio qualities of the absolutely true, strong belief. When this is complete, you will think of your empowering belief in the same way that you think of your other absolutely true, strongly held beliefs. Ensure that your visual and audio qualities of your new absolutely true beliefs and your previous absolutely true beliefs match as much as possible.

Here's the Change The Belief pattern summary:

1. Close your eyes.

2. Think about something that used to be true but no longer is.

3. Notice all the visual qualities of that belief.
    (Location, Distance, Brightness, Clarity, Movie/Snapshot, 3D/Flat)

4. Notice all the auditory qualities of that belief.
    (Location, Distance, Volume, Tempo)

5. Notice all the feeling qualities of that belief.
    (Location, Intensity, Duration)

6. Open your eyes and name three different things
    in the room to clear your mind.

7. Close your eyes.

8. Think about a limiting belief of yours, such as
    "I'm shy," or "I'm not yet confident."

9. Notice all the visual qualities of that belief.
    (Location, Distance, Brightness, Clarity, Movie/Snapshot, 3D/Flat)

10. Notice all the auditory qualities of that belief.
    (Location, Distance, Volume, Tempo)

11. Notice all the feeling qualities of that belief.
    (Location, Intensity, Duration)

12. Open your eyes and name three different things in
    the room to clear your mind.

13. Now that you know the visual/sound/feeling qualities of both beliefs,
    adjust your limiting belief to be like the belief of something that used
    to be true but no longer is. Change all the qualities so that the limiting
    belief becomes a belief that is no longer true but used to be.

I encourage you to practice changing your beliefs and experiences. You'll be
surprised at how easy and effective it is.

Use Expectancy To Your Advantage

What you expect tends to be realized more often than you might think.
Resourceful people have different beliefs than unresourceful people.
Resourceful people expect to be able to find a way to get their outcome.
They expect to be able to easily and naturally form rapport with anyone
they meet. They expect to go for it and if they make a mistake, to learn from
that feedback. These beliefs tend to manifest themselves in reality. Believing
the following ideas will increase your interpersonal skills and personal
effectiveness.

When you meet people and you want to create rapport, hold these beliefs:

- People automatically like you since you are a good person.

- You can easily and naturally meet anyone you choose.

- You can have instant rapport with anyone you choose using
  these techniques.

- You have much more in common than you have differences with any
  person you meet.

- You can learn something from each and every person you
  speak with.

You may be thinking that these beliefs are not necessarily true. And if you
were thinking that, you would be correct. However, we're out to get a result
instead of logically proving what is and is not true. The above beliefs are
useful generalizations that will help you when you believe them. In all interpersonal relations, assume that you can get and maintain rapport. Operate
under the belief that you have far more in common with the person than you
have not in common, and therefore you will easily connect with them.

Defuse Limiting Beliefs With The Power Of Questions

∨ The following method uses questions that are designed to break up limiting beliefs. These questions help you reconnect with your confidence resources. Remember that you have the confidence within you at all times. You have successfully been confident in the past. The key is to summon the necessary confidence whenever you choose.

∨ If you're hesitating or behaving tentatively, ask yourself, "What's stopping me from doing what I want?" Once you have the answer to this question, you can change your frame of mind, your internal dialogue, and your physiology to transform into a state of confidence.

If in fact you do find yourself acting shy, never beat yourself up over it.
∨ Remember that there is a positive intention behind every behavior. That means that the way you were acting served some purpose that ultimately did some good in some context in your past. Figure out what the positive intention of your shy behavior is by questioning, "What is the positive intention of this tentative feeling?" Be silent and allow the genuine answer to pop into your mind. When you get an answer, thank yourself for wanting the best for yourself and politely tell yourself that shy behavior is an outdated way of behaving, and that you choose confidence from here onward. Be good to yourself at all times.

Never ask yourself a question like "Why am I shy?" Asking poor questions like that will only keep you stuck, because your unconscious mind will come back to you with answers about why you are shy, thus reinforcing the shyness even further. That's the last thing you want.

You want to ask questions that reconnect you to your resources of confidence. Ask yourself, "What would it be like if I were feeling unstoppably confident right now?" How would you feel differently right now? How would you look out at the world as a supremely confident person? By merely answering those empowering questions, you will be forced to access a state of confidence, thereby meeting your desired outcome.

What Stops People From Turning Dreams Into Reality

People stop themselves from achieving what they want for various reasons. Being aware of what stops people means we can prevent ourselves from being stopped and thereby live our dreams. What I challenge you to do is systematically go through your life and kick out all the excuse "crutches" that you may have been relying on. I had a number of excuse crutches that I leaned heavily on in my life, and those crutches got me nowhere. Blow out the crutches permanently, and then there is no choice but success. This is one of the rare times when you want to reduce your options to ultimately gain more options in the future. The four major causes of blunted progress √ are: *fear of change, fear of the unknown, fear of success,* and the *fear of failure*.

Fear Of Change

People are habitual creatures. They normally do the same thing over and over. This can be good in some contexts. It simplifies our lives so we don't have to consciously think about driving a car, opening a door, or using a computer. On the flip side, this can be detrimental to our well-being. If we act too much out of habit and become automatons, we lose our conscious choice for what we really want to do. Being confident is a change that people may fear since being confident has an entirely new set of behaviors, attitudes, and values that differ from being shy.

A useful belief is that change is fun and easy. Change means personal growth, and personal growth means you're really alive. It shows you that you are not stagnating.

Sometimes on the outset of a change, it may be painful or seem to have negative effects. Napoleon Hill said, "In every adversity, there is a seed of equal or greater benefit." Always look on the bright side. Think long-term. Dwell on how this can help you. Pretty soon, you'll discover yourself doing this automatically. The more you practice, the easier it gets. How excited would you be to find yourself with a sunnier disposition day in and day out when you always look on the bright side of things?

Fear Of The Unknown

The fear of the unknown does not make much sense as a fear although some people still do it. Life inherently has many unknowns to it. You never know just what might happen. Is it worth wasting your valuable time and energy contemplating what *might* happen?

Of course, you can make provisions to ensure that the worst-case scenario in all situations does not happen. Or if the worst-case scenario should happen, you can minimize the damaging effects. There is a finer distinction here. That distinction is that there is a difference between taking action to prevent or minimize the worst-case scenario and wasting time worrying about something that might happen without taking action. Avoid spending time worrying √ and fearing. Instead, take action and increase your peace of mind.   √

If I can offer you a useful frame of mind as you consider life and the unknown, think of life as an adventure. Or think of your life as a game where you make up your own rules to play by. If you moved through life with those frames of mind, how much more exciting and fun would you naturally make your life now?

Fear Of Success

Some people fear success. It paralyzes people. Successful people have overcome this and that's why they are successful. Some people labor under the delusion that if one becomes successful, they have to move to a different neighborhood, lose all of their friends, and their world as they know it is going to end. Success comes in many forms (marital, spiritual, physical, mental, professional, financial, etc.) and success is wonderful. It is very rewarding, and all people deserve to be successful.

Sometimes people shun success because they think there will be a higher standard set for them and consequently more pressure to perform consistently at that high level. It's true that there will be a higher standard set for them. You should always expect excellence out of yourself. You deserve to perform at a high level no matter what the context.

Avoid playing the "not going to lose" game. Always play the "play to win" game.

Fear Of Failure

Fear of failure stops many people from going after what they want. People tend to dwell on what happens if they fail. They always think about what happens if nothing goes right. When they do that, they picture all sorts of unlikely hypothetical situations and eventually talk themselves out of doing something wonderful.

When people venture outside their comfort zones, they need to focus on the potential benefits and remember why it's important to them to go for it. After all, there is no such thing as failure. There are only results. Some results are better than others. If you get results that you don't like, you'll naturally adjust your behavior based upon the results to persist until you achieve your outcome.

To get past the fear of failure, answer the following questions: If you knew you couldn't fail at something, what would you go out and do? What would you achieve? How would your life be different than it is now? What does the life of your dreams look like? How would it feel to live the life of your dreams? First you must conceive it, then you must believe it, and finally *you will achieve it*. Your initial answers to these questions are what you should pursue. Go for it and make it happen.

Remember that mistakes are the way we all learn. We all make mistakes all the time. The more we make them the better, since that means we're learning faster than if we weren't making any mistakes. The key is to make a lot of them and avoid the catastrophic mistakes. Even if you did nothing and tried your hardest not to make a mistake, it would be impossible, since doing nothing would be a mistake. People are bound to make mistakes, so let's make the most of them. One motto I really like is "Fail Forward Fast." Keep on making the mistakes. Learn from them. Adjust and move on. And then repeat the cycle. Without making mistakes, there is no personal growth. Without personal growth, there is stagnation.

My Experience With Failure

I sure screwed up royally with a company I founded. My partner from college and I started a high-tech company where our principal product was software designed to monitor the number of people who visited a website on the Internet. Having no prior business experience and being underfunded, our business failed despite our best efforts to keep it afloat. We simply made no money because we lacked business experience, had no clue on how to find competent advisors, and did not have a good marketing and sales team.

At the time, we had one major rival in our market segment and they dominated the market. Although they had a great software product, we felt that ours was technically superior to theirs in terms of features. Still, our business failed miserably.

Six short years after my company failed, each of the founders of the other software company had a financial net worth of over one hundred million dollars based upon the valuation of the company. This blew me away, since I was a founder of my company along with my partner. For a moment, I contemplated what might have been. That's a great way to feel regret, something I didn't want to do so I immediately derailed that train of thought.

Do I feel like I failed at the company? No. Do I feel like I lost out on a hundred million dollars? No. Did I kick myself and beat myself up over this? Not a chance. Admittedly, I was frustrated, yet that quickly passed. Following the frustration period, I asked myself what I learned. The lessons I took away from the experience were priceless. And those lessons help me today in my current businesses.

Failure From An Unstoppably Confident Perspective

Confident people are confident because they know that they can get what they want. How do they know this? Because they know they're going to persist until they succeed. Until they win. Until they get what they want. They may have a temporary setback, yet they're going to learn from those, do things differently, and finally achieve their goals. So how do they do this? Well, this reminds me of a story that you may have heard.

A group of frogs hopped about a farm, and came across a bucket of milk that the farmer had inadvertently left behind. They dared each other to jump over the bucket, and they did, over and over until one frog misjudged his jump and fell into the milk. He tried to scramble out of the bucket but the sides were too slick and he still fell back in, and outside he could hear the other frogs laughing at him. Not only was he in danger of drowning, but other frogs that he thought were his friends were laughing about it! He was determined to get out, so he swam and jumped and swam and jumped, and the more he tried, the more they laughed at him. As he did so, all of his motions churned the milk until it became butter, and when the butter was thick enough, the frog had enough leverage to jump out and escape.

What does this teach us? If you want something badly enough, *you will achieve it.* No matter what happens, no matter what anyone says or tells you, even if those that you thought were your friends tell you that "you can't do it," you know that *you can.*

How To Avoid Limiting Yourself

V Empowerment means having more choices or options in this world. The more options one has means the more behavioral flexibility one has. The more behavioral flexibility one has means that one can vary their behavior in more ways to consequently increase the likelihood of achieving their outcomes.

As kids we are perfectly empowered. We come into the world and believe anything is possible because the truth is embedded in our minds, bodies, and spirits from the beginning. Kids actually already have empowerment figured out. They're not aware of guilt, fear, negativity, and embarrassment until some authority figure comes along and indoctrinates them with how to feel all those negative emotions. It's at the same time that self-consciousness gets instilled in young children as well.

One time I went on a camping trip. During the trip, some friends and I decided to go hiking. It was a beautiful, clear, sunny day so I only wore shorts and a tank top. Before I knew it, rain started to trickle down from the sky. And then it began to pour. As the rain fell, the temperature dropped and I began to get really cold and my emotions dropped into negativity and self-pity. My friends and I still plodded onward to the summit. We saw a nice view of the landscape and then descended very quickly. What frustrated me most was being so ill-prepared for the venture. In my negative state, I talked to myself on the inside with words like, "This hiking is awful. I'm NEVER doing this again. I thought I prepared well."

Only later on, when I reflected upon the excursion, did I shift into a more resourceful state. I reversed the generalization that I would never hike again. Had I kept to that negative generalization that hiking is painful and causes misery, I probably would not have hiked again. Too often, people have bad experiences and create generalizations that limit their options. By limiting their options, they limit possibilities for themselves in the world. To this day, I enjoy hiking outside (and I am always well-prepared) since I reversed that negative belief I had formed based on that one isolated incident. The key lesson I took away from my "misery hike" was that I needed to be better prepared for weather conditions.

If you ever catch yourself saying "I'm never doing that again," I sincerely challenge you to rethink that. Would there ever be a circumstance where you would do it again? Is there something that would cause you to try it out again? Always seek to add more options rather than subtract them. The more options you have, the more empowered you will be.

Being Confident About Mistakes

Be confident about your mistakes. Mistakes are simply ways we learn. This is the success and confidence strategy of the go-getters of the world. After each success that they experience, they integrate that success into their identity as further evidence that they are unstoppable. And after each "failure," they think about it simply as a function of their behavior without any personal reflection of who they are as people.

Successful people reinforce their success by congratulating themselves and reinforcing their successes through praise. Unconsciously, you will train yourself to gravitate toward that success and praise. It's a great habit to always treat yourself well and praise yourself when you do well.

Supremely resourceful people take success and make it a part of their being. If we could listen in to their internal dialogue, it would go something like this: "This success further proves that I am capable and it's part of who I am. This demonstrates that I can and do achieve my goals and that I am unstoppable." Imagine how empowering it would be to have an internal dialogue like that.

Many people have their strategies flip-flopped. Instead of integrating their success as a part of who they are, they dismiss it. That is all wrong! Dismiss the mistakes as a function of your behavior but not your successes. People dismiss their successes with such phrases as, "Oh, I just got lucky," or "It was bound to happen sometime," or "It was a fluke." All of those phrases remove from the person any responsibility of taking action and generating the success. Catch these phrases in other people's language and yours, too. Then avoid using these phrases. It wasn't luck. It was *you*.

To get your victories to generalize and occur more often, visualize yourself having the same victories in many different contexts just as soon as you get a major victory. When you've got that winning feeling, it's much easier to imagine yourself in the future having that winning feeling over and over again. Visualizing the victories in different contexts will help you generalize the success into the belief that success is part of who you are and success is not an isolated incident that occurs rarely.

Here's how successful people think about their mistakes:

1. If you make a mistake, remember it's simply a function of what you did, not a part of who you are.

2. Ask yourself what you learned from the mistake.

3. Ask yourself what you will do differently next time.

4. Adjust your behavior based upon what you learned.

Here's how successful people think about their successes:

1. Take the success you experienced and make it a part of you. It happened because you are a successful person.

2. Congratulate yourself and celebrate your success.

3. Ask yourself what you could do even better next time.

4. Go for it and see how much better you can do next time.

The confidence you are rapidly developing is like creating a snowball. At first, you pack the smallest bit of snow in your hands and make it as dense as possible so it sticks together. Then you place the small snowball at the top of a great big hill. Rolling the snowball down the hill, the snowball gets more and more snow and gains momentum. Pretty soon, the snowball is unstoppable and going on its own, getting bigger, faster, and acquiring more snow at a faster rate. That's how your confidence is growing now. You're packing your small snowball and the techniques in this book push that snowball down the hill. With this snowball racing down the hill, you are stepping further and further outside your original comfort zone and you're amazed, surprised, and delighted to find that you enjoy this wonderful personal growth.

Once you adopt the belief that "mistakes are your gateway to learning and a natural part of the process," your confidence will immediately jump. The difference between people who are confident and successful and those who are tentative and do not pursue their dreams is how they view mistakes.

If you want to do something well, it's worth doing poorly at first. For unstoppably confident people, mistakes are simply the way they learn. That is why taking action is virtually always better than not taking action. In taking action, you will either reach your outcome or you will at least learn something so that you can do things better the next time. If someone fails to take action due to fear or doubt or lack of confidence, they learn nothing and are stuck in the same place they were.

The confident mindset says to make as many mistakes as you can as fast as you possibly can. The key here is to correct what you're doing based upon the feedback you listen to at each mistake. By constantly correcting, eventually you will reach your outcome. And when you do succeed, you can develop ways to succeed even better. Furthermore, when you succeed, integrate your success into your identity as a successful person of unstoppable confidence.

The tentative mindset laments that mistakes are bad and wrong and should be avoided. As you think about that, you'll naturally find how ineffective that mindset might be in terms of getting you to go after your dreams. Mistakes are really only a measure of your behavior and NOT personal evaluations of your worth as an individual. Avoid taking mistakes personally. Instead, learn from them and move on.

A Positive Intention Behind Every Behavior

One time, many years ago, I was lighting firecrackers for the Fourth of July and having a great time, like a young kid should. Out of nowhere, my neighbor scaled the fence while blurting out profanities at the top of his lungs, admonishing me to duck down and cease what I was doing at once. Sensing the urgency of the situation although I was seriously confused, I ducked down.

When my neighbor realized that I was only lighting off fireworks, he worked himself out of his frenzy into a calmer state. He told me the story of how he was a war veteran for the U.S. military and when he heard what sounded like gunshots, he instinctively dropped to the ground. That's why he admonished me to do the same. Only when I understood his background did I understand why he did what he did.

Without that automatic instinct to drop down upon hearing gunshot-like noises, he could have died, had he been in war. There was a positive intention behind his behavior, except his behavior was no longer valid for the particular context of me lighting off Fourth of July fireworks. However, his behavior was absolutely necessary in a fighting context, where his life is at stake. This is what it means that for every behavior, no matter how seemingly bizarre, there is an appropriate context for it.

If someone does something that makes you want to react in an unresourceful manner, let the idea that there is a positive intention motivating every behavior come back to you. Upon doing this, give the other person the benefit of the doubt. Even if someone has a bad habit, there is a positive intention behind it. When you were less confident, there was a positive intention behind that. The positive intention most likely was to protect you from getting rejected, because up until now, you did not have the resource strategies that are outlined in this book to have unstoppable confidence. Realize there is no such thing as rejection or failure.

For empowering yourself in your life, a useful belief to hold is this: There is a positive intention motivating every behavior and a context in which every behavior has value. No matter how ridiculous or unresourceful someone's behavior apparently is, there is an underlying positive intention to it or else the person would not do it. If ever you find yourself feeling stuck or wronged by another person, remember that the other person's behavior has a positive intention behind it. Too often, people ascribe a negative intention to another's behavior and emphatically exclaim, "They're out to get me!" Go back to being the reverse paranoid. The reverse paranoid believes the universe is perfect and good and will align to work with you to reach your goals. If someone does something wrong, always mind-read positively. By mind-reading positively, I mean that we can imagine a circumstance or a thinking pattern in which doing whatever action they did would make perfect sense. Give them the benefit of the doubt. Having this idea means to you that you will experience less frustration in the world and cause you to stay resourceful and away from a victim mentality.

No matter how seemingly inappropriate a behavior is, there is always at least one context in which a behavior is useful. For example, if someone shows up late, you might give them the benefit of the doubt and stay resourceful instead of getting angry because you realize that there was a positive intention behind their behavior. And perhaps being late is effective for them. If you want to make a grand entrance and have all the eyes turn toward you as you enter a dinner party or event, it may behoove you to be late. This means that being late can be a good, resourceful skill to have. Realize you have a positive intention driving your every behavior. No matter what you do or how you behave, you are creating experiences that will serve as resources in your future. Perhaps you are working in a profession completely unrelated to your passion. This may lead you to question, "How on Earth is what I'm doing now going to benefit me?" You may not know how it will benefit you until you are actually living your passion, and then you'll be able to look back on your current experience and realize how it has helped you.

Before becoming a real estate entrepreneur, I got my master's degree in computer science and worked as a software engineer for a Fortune 500 company. And all the time I was doing it, I wondered, "How will doing this work serve me in being a real estate investor, public speaker and a writer?" Although I did not know it at the time, I've discovered that the job helped me develop advanced problem-solving skills that are applicable anywhere. By working in a successful corporation, I got a close-up look at how things are done. This is useful to me in creating my own corporations. The only way I make money now is by solving problems and, thankfully, I got good at solving problems in my previous job. Real estate investing and engineering software are completely different, yet some of the overriding skills transfer very well.

Be courageous. I have seen many depressions in business.
Always America has emerged from these stronger and more prosperous.
Be brave as your fathers before you. Have faith! Go forward!

— Thomas A. Edison

the body language of confidence

If we are to have magical bodies,
we must have magical minds.

— Dr. Wayne Dyer

States are your internal pictures, sounds, and feelings coupled with your physiology. Your internal pictures, sounds, and feelings affect your physiology and vice versa. Sometimes people move tentatively or are in the habit of not carrying themselves with confident physiology. This causes people to internally experience a lack of confidence, something we want to avoid. In stressful situations, sometimes people resort to blaming and placating. To do this, they engage in certain gestures of placating and blaming that cause them to go into this state. If they were to alter their behavior by maintaining powerfully confident physiology, their internal state would match that of a calm, cool, and collected person. Being calm, cool, and collected is much more resourceful and effective for solving a problem than blaming and placating ever could be. This chapter outlines some methods for how to move your body to stay confident.

Avoid Wimpy And Blaming Gestures

Confident people avoid placating gestures. These are gestures that someone makes that convey that they are inferior or in some way submitting to another person. In order to have unstoppable confidence, these gestures must be avoided at all times. A classic placating gesture is that of someone shrugging their shoulders with their palms faced upward as if they are pleading, "I didn't do it." This conveys that they are trying to absolve themselves of responsibility from a situation.

Another placating gesture is the shrug, which means that people don't really know what is going on or perhaps don't even care. It does not make any sense to convey to others that you don't care about something. If you do not know about something, simply say it verbally in a matter-of-fact way. People who lack confidence often shrug in an obvious manner and say in a frustrated or annoyed tone that they have got no clue. A lot of times people can find the answer to problems if they would stop for a moment and think about potential solutions instead of giving up so easily and saying they don't know. Henry Ford said, "Thinking is the hardest activity there is to do. That is why so few people engage in it." People who are confident may not immediately have the answer, yet they realize they have all the resources to go get the answer.

When someone asks a question and the immediate response is "I don't know," "I have got no idea," or "I haven't a clue," this indicates to me that these people are not even willing to use their minds to make an educated guess or take it upon themselves to find out. A better response when someone genuinely does not know is to say, "I'm not sure yet." This indicates the truth about the uncertainty of the person and presupposes that they will be sure sometime in the future, as indicated by the word "yet."

The opposite of placating is blaming. Unstoppably confident people do not blame. Blaming means that you are accusing someone of something. The blame frame of mind is a very negative frame of reference that does not empower people. Gestures for blaming people are when someone tightens up and points accusingly at someone else with their index finger protruding while basically declaring, "It's all your fault. It's all your doing." Too many people blame, and it's not useful.

Confident people come from the place of *finding solutions*. They look for options for how to solve problems and create solutions. They move through the world, calmly, coolly, unperturbed by outside events. The difference here is that they manage their emotions and avoid letting their emotions dominate them.

Avoid both blaming and placating gestures. Instead, be who you are, truly unstoppable. An unstoppably confident person who solves problems and gets the job at hand done in an efficient manner. Who or what caused something is irrelevant. The main idea is to solve the problems now and prevent them from occurring in the future. A situation is what it is, and for you to get where you need to go, simply go after it and get it done.

Walk Confidently

Confident people have a confident walk. Inside their minds, it's as if they are saying, "I own this place. I am completely resourceful and successful." As you practice walking confidently, project those good thoughts outward. They will manifest themselves in your body language: head held high, standing up straight, shoulders back, tummy tucked in, and moving through the world with deliberate steps. Feel free to walk at your own pace instead of adopting the speed everyone else is walking. Avoid shuffling your feet or looking down at the ground. You'll notice a difference as you practice your confident body language and projecting your confident intention when you walk.

Steeple For Confidence

Steepling is a gesture that conveys confidence. Steepling is when people press their fingertips together while keeping their palms separate. Each of your fingertips touches the fingertip of the opposite hand. Many unstoppably confident people steeple to exude confidence and therefore the gesture is associated with confidence. Get in the habit of steepling when you want confidence and when you want to convey confidence to others.

There is nothing more dreadful than the habit of doubt.
Doubt separates people. It is a poison that disintegrates friendships
and breaks up pleasant relations. It is a thorn that irritates and hurts;
it is a sword that kills.

— Buddha

mastering your internal voice

Quality questions create a quality of life.
Successful people ask better questions,
and as a result, they get better answers.

— Anthony Robbins

A major influence of your state of mind is your internal voice, the voice you ✓
use when you speak to yourself. There are many ways that you can speak to
yourself, but not all of them will lead you to the powerful confidence and
strength that you want and deserve.

Imagine you have a private stereo in your mind that plays things personally,
just for you. If you put on a CD and found a whining, droning voice coming
through that stereo, constantly cataloguing the failures you've had, or griping
about how hard life is, you'd feel pretty bad, wouldn't you? Wouldn't you want
to turn it down, or get rid of that CD?

Conversely, if you could switch to a rich, warm voice, reminding you about all
the great things you've done in your life, the things that make you happy and
thankful, the goals and dreams that you have, wouldn't that feel *just great*?
Wouldn't you want to listen to it a lot, maybe turn it up to just the right volume
for you to feel it vibrate in your body? Wouldn't you want to have that helping
you make your life wonderful?

This is exactly what we are going to do in this chapter. We are going to take
your internal voice, and no matter how you have been speaking to yourself in
the past, you will learn to use it to positively change you state of mind and
direct your thoughts in resourceful ways. You will *master* your internal voice
so your state of mind becomes and stays *just great*.

Squashing The Negative Internal Dialogue

Many people have a negative internal voice that constantly nags at them. This
negative internal dialogue often puts them down and dwells upon the nega-

tive things in life. Consequently, it's difficult for people to move ahead if they don't first conquer their negative internal voice.

A negative internal voice can cause a negative self-fulfilling prophecy if one lets the voice rule their mind and, therefore, their world. What occurs far too frequently is that the negative internal dialogue discourages someone from doing something. Then, if they even attempt to do something and fail, the internal voice rubs it in. This further drives home the false belief that they cannot do whatever they set out to do. The negative internal voice then gets louder and incapacitates them even further the next time the person wants to step outside their comfort zone. This cycle must be stopped. Considering all of this, how would you like to silence this negative internal dialogue once and for all?

When you're aware of the specific qualities of the negative internal dialogue, you can more easily silence it. First of all, identify the qualities of the negative internal dialogue by answering the questions below.

- Whose voice do you hear criticizing you?
- What direction does the voice come from?
- What is the volume of the voice?
- Does the voice say the same thing over and over?
- Does the voice speak rapidly or slowly?
- What is the tonality of the voice?

Now that you are more consciously aware of the voice than ever before, we can squash it. To do this, consciously choose to change the qualities of the voice. You do this through imagining the same voice with its vocal properties altered.

Sometimes the negative internal voice is that of your parents. Sometimes the negative internal voice is yours. What would happen if you took the voice and made it sound like Mickey Mouse's voice? What would happen if you took the voice and made it one of your favorite childhood cartoon character's voices? What would happen if you took the voice and had it say the same thing only with a clown voice? Don't take my word for it; do it yourself to find out. You might be surprised to discover how quickly an internal voice that used to keep you stuck becomes meaningless when it sounds like Bozo the Clown.

What happens if you change the location the negative internal voice comes from? Notice how this changes things. Put the voice in different locations and different distances away to find how to lessen the impact of it.

What happens when you imagine a volume dial and turn the volume down on the negative internal voice? What happens when you turn up the negative internal voice? Find what works best for you to thwart the impact of the negative internal voice. Most likely, the quieter the voice, the less influence it will have. It's really very simple once you do it. The underlying basis of this technique is the idea of consciously directing your mind instead of just allowing it to work randomly. Here you are consciously directing how you choose to hear the internal voice of yours.

What happens when you speed the voice up so very fast that it's almost incomprehensible? What happens when you slow the voice down to the point it's *deeeeep aaannnnd dissstooorrrrted*? I bet you're feeling better about having more control over your internal voice, and your negative internal voice is having less and less of an impact on you.

Amplifying Positive Internal Dialogue

For everything we did to the negative internal dialogue, we'll do to the positive internal dialogue in reverse. There are a number of things to do to reinforce the internal dialogue and to amplify its effects.

When you hear positive, encouraging words inside your mind, take a moment and silently thank yourself. As you begin to tell yourself positive things inside your mind, reinforce the behavior. The more you reward yourself for acting in the way you want, the more you will find yourself automatically acting the way you want.

Your ideal internal dialogue should be your voice. The reason for this is that you and you alone run your life and make your decisions. If the internal dialogue has a voice of anyone other than you, you are effectively relinquishing your personal power to them. Since you are running your mind and your life, reclaim it by making the internal dialogue yours alone, forever. Simply replace the current "voice of authority" in your life with your own voice coming from that same place of authority within you.

Allow yourself to hear that positive voice resonate within you. Allow it to spread through all parts of your body. Whenever you hear that glowing, positive internal voice, boom it from within you like it's coming from the largest speakers you've ever heard at the loudest volume imaginable. The louder the volume, the more you will feel the feeling coarse throughout your entire being. So when you want to really feel it, crank up the volume!

While your positive internal voice shows up more and more often, sometimes it will give you a positive statement disguised in question form. An example is, "You can do it?" The tonality may be questioning, yet deep down the sentence is a statement. Crank up the power of your internal voice by turning the sentence into a statement: "You can do it." Try this on by repeating it in your mind a few times. Next, make your internal voice even stronger by converting the statement into the exclamation "You can do it!" Listen to how you like that when you repeat it in your mind a few times. Shout this inside your mind! You will shout out the doubt.

The underlying idea is to begin to trust yourself in the same way that the most successful people in the world trust their internal voices and believe in themselves.

Other people will try to project their limits onto you. If you share your dream with someone and they have limiting beliefs, they may try to put their limits onto you or suggest that it cannot be done. All of this accidental bad hypnosis by friends, family, and colleagues can be counteracted by using the following words: "cancel, cancel." If you catch someone giving you a bad suggestion or projecting their limits inside of you, mentally utter the words "cancel, cancel." These words serve to remind yourself to flush those negative thoughts from your mind. The more you pay attention to people's language, the more you realize how many limits people really do project, which in turn will cause you to use "cancel, cancel" often.

Your confidence is growing with each and every technique that you add to your repertoire. The more your confidence grows, the more you will discover how much you want to reconnect with your passions and go after your dreams. In doing this, ask yourself, "If money were no object and I knew I could not fail, what would I do in my life?" The immediate answer to this question is your passion and what you should do with your life. Avoid the fear reactions and any preconditioned negativity that might try in vain to crop up. Stamp all of that out using the techniques you're learning in this book. Find your passion, set your goals, and then take immediate, repeated, massive action that will virtually guarantee your success. Commit to yourself that you will never quit. Remind yourself that you have quit quitting, and move ahead into the life you want and deserve to have, now.

To Get The Right Answers, Ask Quality Questions

Your unconscious mind will simply give you the answers to any question you ask of it. Therefore, it behooves you to ask it good questions so it can give you good answers. The quality of your life is determined by the quality of your questions you pose to yourself in your life.

People often, in a horrible nasal tone, ask themselves, "Why am I always stuck?" "Why does this always happen to me?" "Why do I make the same mistake over and over again?" Those horrible questions only serve to reinforce one's state of being stuck, because the unconscious mind will find answers to those questions. It will come back for all the reasons that "you are always stuck," "why it always happens to you" and "why you always make the same mistakes." Reasons for those negative positions only further entrench your position of being stuck, and that is the last thing you want.

When you ask yourself questions that deliberately affirm your many options and potentials, your unconscious mind will go off and search for an answer for you. Your unconscious mind is designed to simply answer questions, which is why questions such as "Why do I always screw this up?" will only keep you stuck. Your unconscious goes and fetches reasons for you always screwing something up. The essential element is to ask affirming, directed questions. As you do this, maintain a good, resonant tonality by speaking from your chest. It will help if you do this exercise in front of the mirror.

Knowing that your unconscious mind is an answer box is useful, since you can now use it to your benefit. Ask yourself questions that direct your life in the way you want it to go. How easily and naturally will you find the solution to the problem that you need? How quickly and naturally will you be ten times more confident than you are now? I wonder just how soon you'll achieve all of your goals and lead your dream life. I don't know yet just how much pleasure and delight you can have in taking the next action on the path to your dreams. How can I make my relationships with my family and friends and co-workers even better?

Begin right now to ask yourself questions like, "How much fun can I have? How much pleasure can I stand? How much more confidence can I have? How soon will I be ten times more confident than I am right now? How nice will it be to conquer this nice little fear and go after what I want?" All of these questions presuppose that good things are going to happen to you and it's only a matter of time or a question of how much of a good thing you will experience.

Asking yourself those kinds of questions sets your unconscious in motion. It will go out and search for answers to your questions. By asking these quality questions you will get good results in your life. Structure your questions so that your outcome of what you want is a given in the sentence. In asking poor questions, your unconscious would come back with excuses for being stuck. In asking great questions, your unconscious provides you evidence as to how awesome you truly are!

Sometimes during this exercise, that nagging internal dialogue may rear its ugly head. To get rid of the internal dialogue, imagine giving the voice a really, really, ugly, scrunched-up face to the point where the face is disgusting to even look at. Then imagine a boot drop-kicking the face right out of your mind. Serves it right for trying to stop you from getting what you deserve and

sidetrack your success! Isn't that better now? If it tries to come back, the boot
will be right back.

> You cannot always control what goes on outside.
> But you can always control what goes on inside.
>
> — Dr. Wayne Dyer

unstoppable confidence in personal realtionships

Do unto others as they would like to have done unto them.
— Kent Sayre

Ethics, Manipulation, And Integrity

Some people, upon learning the techniques that will follow, think that they may be manipulating others when they use them. These techniques are simply tools, and it's up to the person using the tools what the results will be. Like any other tool, these methods can be used for good or not so good.

These strategies, techniques, and methods are just like water. If you give water to a thirsty man who traversed fifty miles in the sweltering hot desert, you will save his life. If someone on a cruise ship falls overboard into the ocean and does not know how to swim, they can drown very easily. The water is the same water. It's just the context of how the water was used that makes the difference. Use these tools for the good of all people and there should be no problem at all.

Integrity means acting congruently within your own belief and value system. ✓ Therefore, use what you learn in this book with integrity. These tools are very powerful and can be misused if appropriate care is not taken. Use these tools to make people feel wonderful as you get your outcomes.

Your Confidence Mindset

How you perceive people will influence how they perceive you. If you love ✓ people and enjoy their company, that belief will impact your life tremendously. On the flip side, if you dislike people and generally disdain their company, that belief will affect you a lot. The better you can get along with people, the higher quality life you will lead.

Let's discuss the concept of intention. Intention is the subtext of the interaction between individuals. If you intend to connect with someone and project that intent by setting that as a strong outcome before beginning to talk with them, they will unconsciously pick up on this and respond to you more positively. People want acceptance and want to relax and be themselves, free of any judgment. When you set that as one of your outcomes, to allow people to relax and be themselves, they will find themselves automatically more comfortable in your presence. They may not know why, yet they will feel it.

Do the following as an experiment that will show you the influence of your frame of mind. For a week, adopt the frame of mind that people are unfriendly and don't like to meet new people. Imagine that people don't want to be bothered. After temporarily adopting this frame of mind, go out each day or night for a week and try to strike up conversations with strangers. It will be difficult because of your frame of mind. What the thinker thinks, the prover proves. Having that negative frame of mind becomes a self-fulfilling prophecy. Once the week is over, purge yourself of that toxic frame of mind.

The following week, adopt the frame of mind that people are perfectly friendly and they love meeting new, dynamic people such as yourself. Furthermore, you like to get to know new people since you naturally realize you can learn something new from each and every person. You accept people for who they are, allow them to be themselves, and are free from judging them. After permanently adopting this frame of mind, go out each day or night of the week and notice how easily and naturally you converse with strangers while you make new friends all around.

One of confidence's many benefits is how other people are put at ease when interacting with confident people. If someone is uptight and ill-at-ease, you can sense it and it may cause you to be correspondingly uptight. However, when someone is genuinely comfortable being himself, others sense this and consequently let their guard down to where there can be a more genuine interaction since no one is pretending to be someone they are not.

While you do these experiments to prove the influence of frame of mind for yourself, remember to play and have fun. Forget about having any expectations. The only way in life ever to be disappointed is to have expectations. You have to plan in order to be disappointed. Just go and experiment, play, and practice your new skills. Adjust your behavior continually based upon the feedback you receive.

Confidence In Communication

How Do You Sound To Others?

One key to confident communication is having excellent vocal tonality. Vocal √
tonality is the pitch at which you speak. If your voice is very nasal, it will be
very irritating. Irritating is certainly not good when you go to project a confident image and communicate with people. You want tonality that resonates
within a person and causes them to feel good. It makes a big difference that
most people aren't aware of consciously, but it has an effect on all people at
the unconscious level. Speaking with bad tonality is like someone running
their long fingernails down a chalkboard. Personally, I'd rather listen to a
dental drill than listen to someone drone on with nasal tonality.

What's worse is that few people who have a nasal tonality are even aware that
they do. For everyone who does have it, though, help is on its way. One can
improve their tonality through repeated practice. In this exercise, we will place
our hands on a certain body part and place our attention there while we say
things. As a result, we will notice the shift in our tonality with the end of the
exercise having us finish with a deep, resonant tonality. Place your hands on
your nose and say, "This is my nose." The tonality should be nasally now and
mild to very irritating. Move your hands down to your mouth now and say,
"This is my mouth." As you do this, listen for the difference in your tonality
already. Next, place your hands on your throat as you say, "This is my throat."
Hear the change in your tonality yet? Place your hands on your upper chest
and declare, "This is my chest." Notice your tonality becoming more resonant?
Finally, place your hands on your abdomen and say, "This is my abdomen.
When I talk like this, I get a deep, rich tonality that people enjoy." Where your
attention goes, the energy flows, and that is the reason why your tonality gets
better when you concentrate on your abdomen area. If you want someone to
listen to and model, turn on the radio and really concentrate on how the disc
jockeys use their voices. You'll never find a nasally voiced disc jockey for reasons mentioned above.

Here is the Tonality Improvement exercise summary:

1. Place your hands on your nose as you focus your attention there.

2. Say, "This is my nose."

3. Notice your tonality.

4. Place your hands on your mouth as you focus your attention there.

5. Say, "This is my mouth."

6. Notice your tonality improvement.

7. Place your hands on your throat as you focus your attention there.

8. Say, "This is my throat."

9. Notice your tonality improvement.

10. Place your hands on your chest as you focus your attention there.

11. Say, "This is my chest."

Notice your resonant, deeper, more pleasant tonality.

The Wonder Of Smiling

If you want more confidence in the world, smile. To do this, practice smiling to anyone and everyone, everywhere you go! Do this when you're at work, at home, and in the store. No matter where you're at, give someone the gift of a smile. As you get good at smiling and make it a habit, practice making small talk with people. This will cause you to become more adept at conversing and you'll discover your conversations flowing with greater ease than ever before. Ask people how they are doing and find out what they want in life. People love to talk about themselves, and it will make you feel good to really listen to someone intently.

Even for me at the depths of my shyness, smiling was very effective. Being a naturally happy guy, I smiled often at people just because it came naturally. It really is a life-changing habit to develop. What I discovered is that when I smiled at people, they would naturally smile back. In fact, I'd even make a game out of it to smile and see how many other people I could make smile. Sometimes I'd smile a little bit and the other person wouldn't smile so I'd broaden my smile and keep making my smile bigger until they broke out of their stoic facial expression and smiled back. It's quite a great feeling to give a smile. Give as many as you can because they are free, they make you feel good, and the person you smile at will feel good, too. Smiling is quite disarming. The way it works is, people will perceive others with a genuine smile as being authentic, being real, and being trustworthy. More positive traits are ascribed to people that smile than people who do not.

The Platinum Rule

In dealing with people, many have heard of the Golden Rule, but how many know of the *Platinum Rule*?

The Golden Rule: Do unto others as you would have done unto you.

The Platinum Rule: Do unto others as they would like to have done unto them.

When you think about it, the platinum rule obviously makes more sense. If someone feels down and you recognize it, you can proactively make that person feel wonderful.

Overcoming Intimidation

One thing that you may encounter on your journey is intimidation. Many things can cause a person to feel intimidated, including beauty, fame, fortune, and social status. People possessing these and similar qualities can seem intimidating, and once again, it is important to remember that feeling intimidated, like shyness, fear, anxiety and every other emotion, is the result of a mental process.

Remember, who is in control?

You are.

If you ever find yourself dealing with someone and feeling intimidated, recognize the feeling as soon as you feel it. By becoming aware of it and identifying it, you can do something about it. Take a few steps back and look at the big picture overall. The big picture shows that you are two people talking or interacting in some fashion. It's really not such a big deal. They are simply a person in the same way that you are simply a person. When you strip away everything else, the person who used to intimidate you puts their pants on the same way you and I do every day. Remembering this will eliminate intimidation you may have felt in the past, and therefore build the unstoppable confidence within you.

Men often complain about a particular beautiful woman, "Oh, sure I'd like to go out with her but she's beautiful! She is way out of my league." That is utter and complete nonsense. People are people. No one is below or above anyone else. Beautiful women and other people who might intimidate others are simply human beings with beliefs, desires, values, hopes, dreams, fears, and goals like anyone else's. When you think about things like this, doesn't it make it that much easier to interact with people? As you apply these ideas in your life, I think you'll find out for yourself that it does. If I ever feel intimidated by someone, it's due to the fact that I'm focusing on the wrong thing. All of us have extraordinary gifts and if others solely focused on our gifts, they may become overwhelmed and thus intimidated. We're both human beings and we have much, much more in common than we have different.

If I feel intimidated, it's because I'm not only dwelling on their extraordinary gift but I'm also blowing it WAY out of proportion. In blowing it out of proportion, I'm totally exaggerating it and making it larger than life. It's an excellent strategy to feel intimidated and one that far too many people have mastered.

A useful belief in dealing with someone who has the potential to intimidate you is that whenever you meet anyone, you can realize that everyone has at least SOMETHING in common and you can find that in any person you meet. People have much more in common with others than they realize. All people have the same wishes, hopes, dreams, and fears overall. People want to be happy, prosperous, take care of their families, enjoy their lives, and have the freedom to pursue what they want. Furthermore, people want to avoid going broke, avoid sickness, and avoid death for themselves and their loved ones. When you keep these beliefs in mind as you talk to a person, you will discover your connection to others deepen as a result of you projecting that intention of "Hey, we're alike" to the other person.

How To Keep Things In Perspective

If you've ever seen a movie where the camera begins with a close-up shot of a person and then zooms out to include the nearby house and zooms further to the entire neighborhood, the city, the state, the continent, and then looks back at the entire world, then you'll naturally understand the basis for this next technique. This zooming out and zooming in action helps us understand how we fit in. Our surroundings help to put and then keep things in perspective. After all, if we remind ourselves who we are in the entire scheme of things, it's harder to make our problems larger than life, isn't it? This makes what we go through as we live our lives much simpler and less dramatic.

If you are not confident yet in a particular area, put it into perspective. People blow things way out of proportion on a regular basis. They do this unconsciously in their minds. When people worry over something unnecessarily, it's most likely caused by them blowing things out of proportion in their minds. They have taken something and made it more important than life itself. Another way of stating that is that people turn incidental things into a figurative life or death struggle. Blowing things out of proportion is taxing to people in both time and energy lost. They cannot get back that valuable energy and time, and yet for some reason they still blow things out of proportion. It's useless to only think of negative things. Always take caution to prevent disasters in your life, yet the key here is action.

To do this exercise, first read through all of the instructions and then do them. Visualize the entire Earth. Then picture yourself and where you are on Earth. Look at yourself from up above as if you are ten feet above yourself looking down. As you do this, notice how you can see in your periphery your surroundings. Now imagine yourself from a higher perspective to the point where you can see yourself amongst your entire city and view everything together at once. Doing this changes your perspective on things and prevents you from blowing things out of proportion. Continue to zoom upward while looking down at yourself until you can see yourself waving up at you in the sky as you look at your entire region. You notice how this changes the perspective on your problem, don't you? Zoom all the way out until you see your entire country and then see the whole Earth and keep in perspective your size relative to the rest of the Earth. You'll immediately notice a shift in your perception. As you begin to put things in perspective and realize the true significance of them in your life, you will find yourself less stressed out about trivial things.

Another great technique to do is to visualize the timeline of your life. Imagine there is a line of time that spans from your past to the present to your future. You can picture your past off to the left, the present right in the middle, and the future veering off to the right. If something is troubling you or you are lacking confidence about something, put a small dot on the timeline to indicate it.

Now as you remember this problem you have been spending valuable time and energy on, mentally step back from your timeline so that you can see more of it at once. As you do this, notice how much smaller that dot representing your problem becomes. Distance yourself from your timeline to the point where you can view the entire time of your life at once and try to see if you can if strain to see the dot that represents your current problem. Next, superimpose your timeline on the timeline of the universe. Notice how much smaller your timeline is when you compare it to the vastness of the entire life of the universe.

To fully consider your problem in its true perspective, look at all of the time of the universe as you try to see that small dot of a minor problem that used to bother you that is on your timeline. Life is too short to spend your valuable time worrying about frivolous things that in the entire scheme of things really don't matter. Take action and achieve your goals and be done with it.

Here's the Put Things In Perspective technique summary:

1. Imagine you're getting in a helicopter. Zoom around and visit all of your friends and family. Notice that they have problems, goals, hopes, dreams, wishes and fears like you do.

2. Zoom out further in your helicopter and notice all the people in your city and notice yourself as one amongst them. Each of them has problems, goals, hopes, dreams, wishes, and fears like you do.

3. Zoom back into yourself and notice the difference in perspective you have for your problem already.

4. Zoom back out to your friends, your city, your region, and now your state. Notice all the people in your entire state at once and notice how you are one person out of all of them.

5. Imagine yourself getting into a spaceship and zoom out until you can see the entire country of people. And you're just one of them dwelling on this little event in your life. Each and every one of these people have problems, goals, hopes, dreams, wishes and fears like you do.

6. Zoom all the way back in to yourself. Notice how the problem is even further in a more manageable perspective and how it has already changed.

7. Get back in your spaceship and zoom all the way out until you can view Earth in its entirety. Imagine you can see all six billion people of the planet smiling and waving at you. Listen to them say,"Hey, it's no big deal. You are one person of six billion. Keep the perspective reasonable."

8. Notice how the issue/event/problem has changed.

The Look Of Confidence

Confident people are able to look people straight in the eye and tell it like it is. By looking at someone in the eye no matter what you are saying, you will be perceived as being more sincere, genuine, and honest than if you are shifty-eyed and avoiding eye contact. People who lack confidence tend to fail to look at people directly in the eye. This brings about suspicion from the person they are interacting with because most people when they are telling the truth look people directly in the eye. If you have nothing to hide, focus your attention on looking at people in the eye. Not only do you want to look people directly in the eye, you can practice feeling good while you do it.

If right now you have a tendency to avoid eye contact, that's just fine as a starting point. After you do the following exercise, you will discover how easily and naturally you can do it. By the end of this exercise, you will have formed the beginning of a habit. The difference between confident people and shy people, in summary, is that confident people have confident habits that cause them to behave confidently. In the same way, shy people have habits that force them to act shy.

Eye-Contact Exercise

This exercise is designed to gain you more confidence by being able to "be present" with someone and look them straight in the eye. You'll need a partner for this exercise, and a great partner would be a supportive friend, spouse, or relative. Read through the entire directions before you do the exercise. By doing this exercise you'll naturally find yourself breaking through limits as your confidence rises to unprecedented levels.

Set an outcome for yourself for what you want to get out of this exercise. One good outcome is to look anyone in the eye, anytime you choose, and tell them what you want and feel at ease while you're doing it.

The exercise directions are as follows. Get a timer that will signal the end of five minutes. What you are going to do is sit across from your partner in complete silence and "be present" with them by being silent and looking at them straight in the eyes.

As you do this exercise, you may have certain urges to laugh or look away. That is fine, and it means you have an opportunity to break through previously held limits. Stay with the exercise and continue to look at the person in the eye. Meanwhile, they are doing the same with you. Having this skill means that you can confront any person and be there with them to accomplish your outcome. Your direct eye contact with another person means you're neither superior nor inferior. You are equals communicating on level ground.

If you do laugh or glance away, your partner will gently say, "Stop. Be present. Start again." Similarly, if they laugh or glance away, you give them the same instruction. You continue on like this for the entire five minutes. We are taught that it's impolite to stare, and we should not. That may be useful in contexts, yet it's also useful to be able to confront someone and be present with them.

Do this exercise with your partner as many times as you feel you need to in order to be able to look at someone. Pretty soon, what you'll discover is that it is really very simple to look at someone and continue to do so. You will no longer be intimidated by direct eye contact.

The real world is the true test to gauge how far you've come. After doing the exercise, practice it in the real world and notice how easily you do it. I wonder just how surprised you will be to find yourself doing it automatically. Others will react positively to your new confidence. This eye contact that you've learned is not designed to intimidate, but to foster better communication through honesty and openness.

The Magic Of Touch

People who are well liked and who are confident put others at ease when they are around. Confident people let others relax and be themselves because those with confidence are being themselves. One method by which ✓ they put others at ease and convey a warm feeling is by utilizing the power of touch. People crave making a connection to other people, so touching and being touched by others is one powerful way we do it. No matter whether the touch is a handshake, a congratulatory pat on the back, or a warm hug, people respond to touch.

An example to demonstrate the power of touch was a study conducted with waitresses and how touching customers influenced their tips they earned. The first group of waitresses touched each customer as they ordered their item off the menu. The second group of waitresses acted just as friendly in demeanor yet they did not touch the customers at all. What the researchers found was that the waitresses who touched their customers earned fifty percent higher tips than waitresses who did not. What this shows is how unconsciously the customers perceived the touching waitresses as more likable, confident, and open.

Think about someone you know who is warm and friendly. Chances are, they make the human connection to others more powerful through the use of touch. As you think about how connecting it is to touch and be touched, you might imagine all of the different contexts and ways in which you can apply this in your own day-to-day life to skyrocket your confidence and connect at a deeper level with others.

Finally, though, a word of warning. In this currently litigious climate of avoiding sexual harassment, men need to be extremely cautious if they are going to touch a woman, especially if it's in the workplace, so that they can avoid those issues. You need to be responsible and understand your company and their policy on touching. It's also important to understand how the recipient of the touch may perceive it. You never know how someone is going to perceive a touch. Now that's unfortunate, yet that's the way it is. Apply touch judiciously and appropriately and, of course, use your common sense.

Interpersonal Skills

Interpersonal skills are fundamental to unstoppable confidence. Simply knowing these interpersonal skills will dramatically increase your confidence. Because you know how people work, you will naturally be able to relate to anyone and everyone very easily by the time you finish this book.

Stop for just a moment and think about your best friend. Perhaps you can even picture that person clearly in your mind. As you keep that person's image in your mind, I want you to notice what specifically it is you like about them. Chances are, you like them because of the following three universal characteristics that make people like one another. The basis of your friendship with your best friend and all friendships are:

- Similarity
- Cooperation
- Praise

Similarity

Similarity means people like people who they *perceive* as being like them. Your best friend and you have things in common. They may include similar attitudes, beliefs, hobbies, goals, and dreams. More likely than not, you like to do similar things. Furthermore, you and your best friend probably have similar dislikes as well. We will use the similarity principle to enhance our interpersonal relations and thereby increase our own personal confidence. Later on, we will make a distinction between true similarity and perceived similarity and how this affects interpersonal relations.

Cooperation

The next ingredient to making someone like someone else is cooperation. It ✓✓ is an absolute necessity. Without cooperation, there can be no basis for friendship. People who cooperate with you, participate in activities with you, and who generally agree with you are undoubtedly more likable to you than people who do not. If someone you consider your friend decides one day to stop returning your phone calls, canceling appointments on you, and generally becomes uncooperative with you, it would obviously be difficult to maintain the friendship no matter how similar you both are.

Praise

Praise is the final ingredient to making one person like another. The impor- ✓✓ tance of praise is intuitively obvious. People like to be praised. We like to be ✓ complimented and recognized for our achievements. Often times at work, employees become disgruntled not because they are not compensated well monetarily but because their hard work goes unrewarded with recognition. Just as praise unites people in harmony, put-downs and insults divide people. It is much harder to like someone who puts you down than someone who consistently praises you. If your best friend only insulted you and put you down, you would quickly dissolve that friendship.

Utilizing The Principles Of Similarity, Cooperation, And Praise

We can harness the power of our knowledge of similarity, cooperation, and praise to magnify our connections to others. People can easily cooperate by being agreeable to on another and working together in win/win situations. In the same way, people can praise one another to create a strong foundation for friendship. We will focus on increasing our *perceived* similarity to someone ✓ else in this section. For example, when people are in a state of deep rapport, when they see eye-to-eye, when they speak the same language, and when you feel they are on the same wavelength, they do certain things. One thing they do is match one another both verbally and nonverbally. By doing what people who are in rapport do, we can duplicate the state of incredible rapport with whomever we're communicating with. It makes no difference whether two people consciously or accidentally match one another verbally and nonverbally, because the results are the same.

Instant Rapport Through Mirroring

When two or more people are in rapport with one another, an interesting thing occurs. Their body physiology (i.e., their body language) becomes similar and they begin to match one another. How can we use this to our benefit? We can consciously match someone else's body language in order to increase our *perceived* similarity to them. While increasing the similarity to them, you simultaneously lessen the differences between yourself and them. This technique is called *matching* or *mirroring* because you will become a mirror image of them.

When I first learned this technique, I confused it with mimicking. Mimicking is something that young children do to their parents to annoy them. We are not mimicking another individual. Instead, we are increasing our similarity to them by mirroring their body language, which will engender a greater understanding of their point of view. Mirroring is actually more respectful than doing nothing at all since you are doing whatever it takes to understand them from their perspective.

The way to mirror/match someone is to use the same body posture as them. As they move, you move with them. Be sure as you do this that you allow for a certain lag time so that your matching of them does not creep into their conscious awareness. Lag time is the time it takes from the time they move until the time you respond and move accordingly. The idea is to gain rapport at an unconscious level with them. The effect on them will be to feel that you are similar to them, although they are not quite sure why. As your rapport deepens, you can trim the lag time until pretty soon you are moving exactly with the person. Rapport is like a dance where two people dance together and one leads and one person follows. Up until this point, you've been involved in the dance and only have been following.

After sufficient rapport has been established, you now have an opportunity in the dance of rapport to lead. To begin leading, move your body into a new position and see if the other person follows you. When they follow you, you know now that you are in fact leading. If you move and for some reason they do not follow by matching you, go back to mirroring/matching and build up the rapport further. While you lead nonverbally, you can match/mirror people in other ways.

In addition to matching body language, you can match people's breathing, too. Like matching, this will serve to unconsciously synchronize you and the other person and facilitate an increase in rapport. To match someone's breathing, watch their shoulders. Shoulders rise on the inhaling of a breath and fall on the exhaling of a breath. People exhale as they are talking so you can remember this to match someone's breathing as they speak. The more similar you are to another person, the deeper rapport you will create. This means that the more behaviors of the other person you match/mirror, the deeper the rapport will be.

Synchronizing with someone's breathing is especially easy if you are touching them. If you have a significant other or a close friend you are sitting close to, you can actually feel them as they inhale and exhale. This makes matching their breathing much easier as you only have to feel where they are in the inhale/exhale cycle and match that.

When I first learned this, I excitedly could not wait to try it out to see the results for myself. I was riding in the back of a car after a late night with some friends. One of my friends was sitting right next to me and he slumped over in a deep sleep. Because we were all cramped in the back seat, I could feel him breathe and he could feel me breathe, although he was not conscious of it since he was asleep. I began matching his breathing. When he inhaled, I inhaled. When he exhaled, I exhaled. After about five minutes, I decided to see if I had established unconscious rapport to the point where I could lead him. I gradually increased my breathing. And much to my surprise and delight, he followed, although he was still deep asleep. I continued to increase my breathing and he continued to follow. Finally I sped up my breathing so that we were nearly panting together, deep in rapport. At this point in time, he exploded from his sleep as he exclaimed, "Kent, what are you doing?" He did not know why he was awake at that time except he felt out of breath. Slowly, his breathing returned to normal as I chuckled inside about how well it worked to match him and then lead his breathing.

Now while I use a non-serious example to demonstrate my point, you can use matching to increase your rapport and intimacy in any human interaction. Another example of my practicing mirroring/matching is as follows. After learning how to match/mirror, I used it with everyone and with one woman in particular. She was an acquaintance and we chatted infrequently, and one day she stopped by to talk. Practicing what I learned, I began talking to her as I matched/mirrored her body posture. For a marathon thirty minutes, I matched all of her motions she made in her body language. Finally, I decided that I had to go for it and see if I could lead her. In the middle of a sentence, I immediately began nodding my head vigorously for no other reason than to test if she would follow. I began nodding up and down, up and down, up and down, without any rhyme or reason to what I was doing. As a result of our deep rapport, she followed right along with me. Here I was, speaking something halfway nonsensical and nodding vigorously for no reason at all and she was doing the same since we were in the dance of rapport. Just as suddenly as I had started nodding and she followed, she gets a confused look on her face as if to ponder, "Why on Earth are we nodding like this right now?" A few seconds later, she stopped nodding and asked me why we were nodding so much. I shared with her the idea of matching/mirroring that caused us to enjoy a good laugh together. Later on, I began matching her again to reestablish the rapport that I had broken by over-nodding. By leading too strongly too soon, you will break rapport with someone and need to regain it by matching/mirroring again.

Here is a list of nonverbal behaviors you can match/mirror in another person:

- Facial expressions
- Body posture
- Eye blinks
- Hand gestures
- Breathing
- Muscle tension/relaxation

Rapport With Groups

Now that you understand how to form rapport with people on a one-to-one basis, you might find it useful to form rapport with an entire group. The way to form rapport with an entire group, because you cannot very well match every person's body language and vocal qualities, is to find who is the leader of the group. In every group, no matter how subtle it may be, there is a leader. You will find out who the leader is of the group, gain rapport with them, and that rapport will transfer to the rest of the group as the followers follow the leader right into rapport with you. A good way to identify the leader is to ask, "Why is the group here today?" All of the followers will turn and look at the leader to answer. When you get the answer, you'll naturally be aware of who the leader is of the group. From there, you can match the leader and develop rapport with the entire group.

Nonverbally Matching A Person For Rapport

The level of *perceived* similarity between you and the other person is directly proportional to the rapport you will experience. The greater level of rapport you experience, the more freedom you will have to relax and be your own confident self around them. As well as matching someone's breathing, you can match their hand gestures. When the other person is talking, notice how they gesture. No matter whether someone has wild, demonstrative gestures, or slight, precise hand gestures match them when it is your turn to speak by speaking with the same gestures. I don't care if it feels awkward or it's outside your comfort zone. You are not matching them for you, you are matching them in order to better understand them and increase communication. You are doing whatever it takes to do that, and that is magnificent.

The basic rule of rapport is to do what they do regardless of whether you feel comfortable doing it or not. You are increasing your similarity to them and understanding how they see the world. Matching means you are being respectful to the other person. A good rule of communication is to remember that you are responsible for your message to be communicated. That means that you need to do whatever it takes to get your message across. Nonverbally matching someone can help facilitate this and increase the chances that the person you are talking with receives your message the way you intended it. If the other person does not get your message, it's not up to them to make sure they get it. As an excellent communicator, it's up to you to ensure they get your message loud and clear.

Facial expressions are another great way to match/mirror someone and develop greater rapport. Smiling, frowning, raising of the eyebrows, or any other facial expression can be matched. To get really specific, you can even match someone's muscle tone. If they are uptight and stressed out, you can match that by tightening yourself up. If they are loose and relaxed, you can relax yourself to be with them. Suppose you match someone who is tense. You can develop great rapport with them and then begin to lead them by gradually relaxing. If the rapport is sufficient, they will follow you and consequently relax.

The best way to get someone to change emotional states is to match the emotional state, gain rapport with the person, and then lead them into a new emotional state. This is why people tend to get angrier when someone tells them in the calmest, most peaceful voice to calm down. Customers who complain about something get infuriated when someone on the other line tells them to take a deep breath and relax. Customer service agents who know this material will match the customer by empathizing with them in the same tonality and body language how they have an absolute right to be angry, frustrated, or whatever. Following this, the customer service agent has rapport established and can then shift into a calmer, more resourceful state that allows the problem to be solved.

Verbal Matching To Enhance Rapport

You now understand how to create rapport by nonverbally matching someone. What we've found is that you can further deepen rapport by matching someone verbally as well. Typical verbal behaviors to match are someone's voice tone, the rate at which they speak, and the words that they use. If someone speaks really rapidly, you don't want to speak really slowly to them. You want to match them by keeping up with their rate. If someone speaks slowly, you don't want to speak really rapidly to them. You want to speak at the rate they are speaking. If you discover someone using the same word over and over again, it's most likely a word with some significance. To increase the rapport, use that word with them and watch the rapport increase. One of my personal words is "fun." I use the word quite often. If someone is talking with me and they use that word often, I feel like they understand me and our rapport really increases.

Listen to people's key words that they say over and over again. I like to call them their "trigger words." It's their hot buttons, if you will. What fires them up about life? When you hear these words, use them back. Use them in all contexts and notice how your rapport skyrockets.

My trigger words are sprinkled throughout this book. If you were to meet me and speak to me using some of the more prevalent words that you see consistently in this book, you will notice me go into a state of delight and our rapport will skyrocket. Some of my trigger words are: "unstoppable," "fun," "powerful," "delight," and "awesome."

Here's an example of how to match someone's trigger words. The conversation is between a painter and his friend.

A painter may say, "I like my art because it's expressive and very freeing. I get to be myself. I paint landscapes that are breathtaking and very open. It allows me to express myself in a way that I didn't get to before. Painting is liberating because I can see the beauty of things around me and express them to others."

The friend can match the numerous trigger words by saying, "That makes sense. I understand where you're coming from. It seems to me like it would be very liberating to be able to really let loose and express yourself to others. To be able to see the true beauty in things to the point where it takes your breath away is really a great treasure. I can see why you like painting so much."

The result of this communication will be that rapport has deepened since the friend matched many of the trigger words the painter used when discussing his passion for painting. Elicit someone's passion, listen for their trigger words, and then speak to them using their own words. You will be amazed at how quickly you develop excellent rapport.

Here is a list of the verbal qualities you can match in a person for greater rapport:

- Tone of voice
- Speed at which they talk
- Number of pauses per sentence

- Trigger words
- Inflection (Questions, Statements, Commands)
- Volume of voice

Build Rapport Verbally By Parroting

Parrots are interesting birds because they repeat certain words or sentences that are said frequently enough. What's amazing is a parrot's uncanny ability to match the tonality, tempo, and exact words that are said. By acting like a parrot, we can increase rapport. When someone is speaking and they pause, repeat the last few words of their sentence right back to them. Repeat the exact words that they said. Avoid changing the words around. Their words have special significance to them or they wouldn't have chosen them that way. If you repeat back other words, it lessens rapport because different words have different meanings. Be like the parrot and repeat back the exact words. You'll discover how easily this causes a greater sense of rapport. Parroting validates that person's point of view and demonstrates to them that you are listening. People like to have their point of view validated and they enjoy being listened to, which is why parroting works so well.

Fred: How are you doing today?

Carolyn: Excellent. I had a flat tire on the way to work but I made it here all right.

Fred: You made it here all right. How has your workday been since that?

Carolyn: Yeah. It's been pretty hectic around the office. I've got a team meeting this afternoon at 4.

Fred: You've got a team meeting at 4. Uh-huh.

Carolyn: Yeah, I'm really looking forward to it. The product should be unveiled here really soon.

Fred: Really soon.

Carolyn: Next week is our scheduled launch. We've been working really hard to get this project going.

Fred: Next week. You must have been working really hard to get this project going.

The parroting is delivered as a mere echo of what the person previously said with the key points echoed back to the person. The speaker, upon hearing her own words parroted back to her, will either vocally say "yeah" or just say "yeah" inside her mind (i.e., nonverbally). Saying "yeah" develops agreement, and when people are in agreement, they are generally in an excellent state of rapport.

As stated earlier, avoid something called *active listening*. In active listening, listen to someone and then change around what they said by putting it into your own words and then spewing it back at them. By changing the words, you change the meaning and distort their true message that they wanted to convey. Avoid this.

Nod And Lean Forward For Greater Rapport

People who are masterful communicators nod as they are listening to others. In doing this, they open others up to relax and share whatever is on their minds. The next time you are talking with someone, continually nod to open them up for sharing. To practice this, get a partner and have a conversation with them. Say as little as possible and nod as often as you appropriately can. This is what effective communicators do, and by modeling effective communicators, your confidence in interpersonal skills and thus in yourself will dramatically increase.

Disinterested communicators lean back and slouch. Excellent communicators lean forward and are interested in what the other person is saying as if they are hanging on each and every word said. In this exercise, lean forward as you nod along with the other person.

As you're talking with your partner, throw in the following phrases at the appropriate pauses and discover how this keeps people talking. I've kept people talking thirty minutes at a time without saying anything else just by nodding, leaning forward, and interjecting these phrases at the appropriate times.

Here are some key phrases to help keep a person talking and increase rapport:

- Uh-huh.
- Yes.
- Go on.
- Tell me more.
- That makes sense.
- I understand.
- Sure.
- Yeah.
- I see what you are saying there. (if they are using visual words)

- I hear what you are saying. (if they are using "sound" words)
- That feels right to me. (if they are using "feeling" words)

Ask Open-Ended Questions

When you realize that you can talk to anyone, anywhere, anytime, you will have more confidence in yourself than ever before. A secret to being a great conversationalist is knowing how to ask questions and show genuine interest in the other person. Quite simply, ask open-ended questions.

Open-ended questions are questions that require more than a simple yes/no response to them. They require the person answering to elaborate and describe what they are thinking. Closed-ended questions do not further develop conversations since they are usually one-word answers. If someone repeatedly responds to you with one-word answers, there's not much to work from to develop the conversation.

An example of a closed-ended question and response is:

Fred: "How are you doing today?"

Eileen: "Fine."

An example of an open-ended question and response is:

Fred: "If anything were possible, what would you most like to be doing right now?"

Eileen: "I have a passion for sailing. I would love to be sailing my boat around the world with my friends. I've been sailing before and I loved it. I can't wait to go again."

You can see the difference between open- and closed-ended questions. They elicit entirely different responses. As you ask these open-ended questions, be sure to listen intently to what the person is saying. While you are listening to someone, use the other methods taught in this book to develop even greater rapport. You can nod and lean forward, parrot their words back to them, match them nonverbally, and use their trigger words. Doing all of this at once may be cumbersome at first. Therefore, practice each skill individually and when you've mastered them, begin to combine them for even better rapport with others.

Stop Mind-Reading

Mind-reading is pretending to be able to read someone's mind and understand their internal state without communicating with them. People mind-read often, which is, unfortunately, to their detriment. Sometimes, people will mind-read about what others think of them. I know I've done this from time to time. And you may have too. People who mind-read are really pretending they are psychic and they can read the thoughts of others without effectively communicating with them. What someone thinks in their mind could be completely different than what you might be mind-reading of them. If a friend fails to call you back or a customer does not get back to you immediately, they might not be interested, or they might have accidentally forgotten. There are many different potential causes for everything and the only way to verifiably know is to ask someone.

For the next week, practice becoming aware of yourself if you are mind-reading. If you automatically assume something about someone else's private thoughts, stop and ask yourself, "How do I know? Have I asked them or have they communicated this to me? Are there alternate possibilities of why they are doing a certain behavior?" When you are aware that you are mind-reading, stop at once.

Fortunately, we can mind-read in a good way. I know that I just told you that mind-reading is something that is less than useful and does not lead to good communication with everyone running around reading one another's thoughts. However, when you mind-read positively, it can be very useful. When I was overcoming my shyness, I had difficulty meeting strangers and, in particular, beautiful women. I used to mind-read and say, "She won't like me. She wants to be alone." This led me to be shy, fear rejection, and be incapacitated in my shyness. And then I decided I had enough of mind-reading negatively. From this point on, I would avoid mind-reading, or if I were going to mind-read, I would do it positively.

I figure if you are going to mind-read, you may as well do it positively. And when I began doing this, my confidence immediately swelled up. I would mind-read people who I wanted to meet with these being "their" thoughts: "I hope he[me] comes over and talks to me. I sure would like to meet a nice, friendly, easy-going guy right about now. How nice would it be for him to come over?" When I thought like this, it more often than not automatically caused me to approach people and meet them. Use mind-reading to your benefit.

How To Respond Resourcefully To Criticism

Now that we've taken care of mind-reading and we are avoiding that now, we will learn how to respond resourcefully to criticism that others have actually said to you or about you. If someone is stepping outside of what others are normally doing and following their dreams and pursuing their passions, there will be criticism. It doesn't matter whether that person deliberately wants to hold you back or not — the effect of the criticism can be the same if you do not respond resourcefully to it. Usually criticism of someone going after their dreams signifies an element of jealously or element of ignorance in the critic. Otherwise, they would be supportive and cheer you on. If a go-getter begins to do things differently and really goes after it, that means the people around will have to cope with change, and few people embrace change.

Recognize before you go after your dreams that you're putting yourself out for ✓ criticism. Avoid letting that stop you and instead just understand that it will be ✓ there whether warranted or unwarranted. Two resourceful responses to the ✓ criticism are either ignoring it altogether or filtering through the criticism in the hunt for valuable feedback. Make a distinction between the kinds of criticism you receive. The first kind of criticism will be people who are trying to tear you down in order to feel better about themselves. The second kind of criticism is by people who mean well and do in fact have good intentions in wanting you to improve. Remember that people treat you how you've taught them to treat you. For people giving you destructive criticism, inform them that they need to correct their behavior.

In order to respond resourcefully to criticism, there must be some distance between you and the criticism so that you can prevent yourself from taking it personally. As you listen to criticism, imagine that you are surrounded by a thick glass barrier in between you and all the criticism and that the glass barrier absorbs any negativity or negative emotions. Only the useful, positive content of the message seeps through the glass barrier. Imagine that this glass barrier repels any and all negativity while still allowing useful feedback to come through and you to receive it. Other people may see and hear things differently and therefore have good suggestions for you on how to improve, which is why you need to be able to receive positive, constructive criticism.

Teach people how to give you good feedback. Good feedback comes in the ✓✓ form of a sandwich. The structure is this: praise for something done well, give ✓ suggestions for improvement, and give more praise for other things done well. By following the feedback sandwich, others feel good and still get useful ideas on how to improve. In giving constructive criticism, the more specific the suggestion for improving, the more useful to you the suggestions will be. The constructive criticism should center on how you can improve next time instead of dwelling upon what you did not do so well at this time around. Give others feedback in this way and expect the same from them. You'll be far more effective than you imagined.

You can learn something new from each person with whom you speak.

— Kent Sayre

twenty explosive techniques for unstoppable confidence

First comes thought; then organization of that thought into ideas and plans; then transformation of those plans into reality. The beginning, as you will observe, is your imagination.

— Napoleon Hill

Changing Your State To Confidence NOW!

It's very important to become aware if and when you are not as confident as you desire. If you're not as confident as you want, it's a direct consequence of running a non-confident process through your mind. One of the major steps ✓ in gaining more confidence is being aware of when you're lacking confidence. The reason for this is because you have to be aware of something before you can change it. When you're aware that you're not being confident, you can change it. It will no longer be a given that you're shy or tentative or whatever label you previously used to describe yourself.

As you become conscious of what you're doing inside your mind with respect ✓ to confidence, pay particular attention to how you're talking to yourself inside. If you have a limiting, negative internal voice with bad tonality nagging at you, I'm sure you naturally realize how it can instantly stop you dead in your tracks when you really want to go for it.

Like paying attention to how you talk to yourself inside, notice what sort of pictures you make inside your mind. When I was locked in my dungeon of shyness, whenever I wanted to go out and meet a woman, I would make a big picture of women rejecting me and laughing at me before I even said hello. With me making those pictures in my mind, I was completely paralyzed with fear and took no action. Instead, I watched opportunity pass me by only to regret it every time. What you hear and see internally impacts how you feel. And how you feel ultimately either frees you to take action or shackles you to hold you back.

If you want excellent feelings, you have to see and hear excellent things.

This is easy because you're in control of your own mental processes. Now, understanding that you have control is very powerful because that means you can change them, so whenever you're acting shy, you realize that it's a process and you can change that process.

If you find yourself acting in a tentative or shy way, here is what to do:

Interrupt The Process:

Imagine a police officer springing up inside your mind, holding a red stop sign, and he shouts out in an authoritative tone as loud as he can, "STOP!" With this image that you hold in your mind, you'll find yourself immediately stopping that process.

Shift Your State:

Once you stop the process, you can change directions and go for a confident process. At the same time, immediately shift your state. Change your state. Have excellent physiology. Head up, shoulders back, stomach tucked in. Put that smile on your face and feel good. Just like that.

Change The Process:

Picture yourself clearly succeeding wildly. Blow the picture up in size until you really feel the intensity of your success. Alter the picture by making it super bright and very close. Doing this increases the intensity of the feelings you get as you look at the picture. Tune into your own voice telling you how unstoppable you are. Be sure to make that voice overwhelmingly loud.

If you find yourself slipping into old patterns of being shy: notice what you're doing, stop it immediately, and start using the techniques found in this book to alter your state.

You Have All The Resources You Could Ever Need Within You

You and I have all the resources we could ever need to be incredibly successful and unstoppably confident in our lives. Many times people discount how resourceful they really are. For example, there have been previous times in your past when you were absolutely confident. You may even consider some of those episodes of unstoppable confidence in you right now. To have unstoppable confidence in the future, your key is to be able to summon those confidence resources at will to get the results you want. You did it successfully in the past, which means you can do it successfully any time. It is only a matter of practice before you have that confidence whenever you choose to switch it on.

Remember a time when you were unstoppably confident in the past. Become aware of what specifically you see, hear, and feel inside as you re-experience what it's like to be completely confident. See what you saw, hear what you heard, and feel that confidence through your entire being. One method to unlock the confidence within you at any time is to go back into the confidence state by reliving past episodes when you were truly confident.

There is a structure to your confidence experience in the same way that there is a structure to a building. There are certain qualities that you see, hear, and feel in a building that inform you what building you are in. Similarly, there are certain qualities of what you see, hear, and feel when you are in a confident state. While you maintain your confident state of reliving a past time when you were confident, become aware of the following visual qualities:

- What size is what you see?
- Do you see a picture or a movie?
- Is it in 3-D?
- Is there a border around it?
- How clear or fuzzy is it?
- How bright is it?
- How close is it?
- Is it in color or black and white?
- Where is it located?

Furthermore, become aware of the following sound qualities:

- What do you hear?
- How loud is it?
- What is the tempo?
- What is the pitch?
- What direction does the sound come from?

Following that, become aware of the following feeling qualities:

- Where does the feeling begin in your body?
- How intense is the feeling?
- What direction does the feeling come from?
- How long does the feeling last?
- What would intensify the feeling?

By altering the visual, sound, and feeling qualities of confidence, you can actually amplify your confident state. Practice playing around with changing all of these different qualities and notice the resulting effects on your confident state. This means you can build an even more confident state once you find the qualities that work best for you.

As you relive your past confident experience and become aware of all the visual, sound, and feeling qualities to that experience, realize that you can use these same qualities to program yourself to have unlimited confidence in the future. The way to do this is by imagining yourself in the future where you will need unstoppable confidence and in imagining your future confident self, adjusting what you see, hear, and feel to match your past experience of confidence. Your mind will encode your future confidence in the same way as your past instances of confidence and naturally draw you to being confident when the future arrives.

You are literally programming your mind to have unstoppable confidence in the future. When the future arrives, your mind will act as if you've already experienced that experience before and give you unlimited confidence. The reason for this is because the mind does not make a distinction between what is real and what has been vividly imagined. Real-time scans of the brain reveal that whether you take a physical action or vividly *imagine* doing it, the same areas of your brain are activated. You can take advantage of this by programming your own mind *in advance*.

Rapid Fire Confidence At Will

Many who have studied psychology will be aware of the groundbreaking experiments conducted by the animal behaviorist Ivan Pavlov to determine the power of stimulus-response conditioning. He noted that dogs salivate when they eat, so he paired a unique stimulus, the shining of a light, with presenting a dog with a meal. Pavlov would turn on the light immediately before giving the dog food, and after several rounds of this, the dog would salivate when the light was turned on but no food was presented. Prior to this pairing, shining the light had no effect on the dog's salivation, but after the stimulus (the light) had been paired with the response (salivation) the dog would reliably salivate when a light was shone.

The phenomenon of stimulus-response conditioning has come to be known as "anchoring" in many circles, and has been applied to phobia treatment, motivation, and other areas of personal development. The beauty of anchoring is that it can be very simple and easy to do for yourself. All through this book we have been using mental techniques to generate strong, confident states. Now, it's all very well to do this when you have the time, but what about when you'd like to get into that state in an *instant*?

This is where anchoring comes in. When you get yourself into the state of being confident and alive, motivated and strong, you can easily pair that state with a stimulus of your own. Many people like to use a special piece of music, maybe a song you like right now, or a piece of music from your past. If you want to do this, pick a piece of music that matches and even evokes the state you want to anchor, like "Eye of the Tiger" or the *Chariots of Fire* theme. Pick out one of your favorite confidence techniques and do it along with the music, and do this over and over again, and you will find that just listening to that music immediately plunges you into that state.

You can even anchor states with *internal* stimuli. As you think about it now, you will realize that any image that automatically puts you into a certain state is already an anchor. For some people, just thinking about the smiling face of their spouse puts them in a romantic state. Thinking about a happy baby is enough to make many people melt with tenderness. All of the imagery in the mental techniques we have been learning is designed to tap into that natural power, to activate the emotional circuitry of your brain and body to produce the confident states you want. Once you have that state, you can pair it with outside stimuli like music or pictures, or you can associate it with internal stimuli like imagined pictures, sounds, or feelings.

Anchors can be set to have an external stimulus to trigger your confident state or to have an internal stimulus. If you have an anchor with an internal stimulus, it's completely under your control because it's something you see, hear or feel inside your mind at any time. Consequently, internal stimulus anchors are more versatile because you can use them wherever you are without needing external stimuli.

A great internal anchor of mine that I want to pass on so that you can make it yours is the following scene. After you imagine it a few times, you'll naturally associate what you see and hear inside your mind with a powerfully confident state. Picture a jet-black puma at the top of a glorious canyon, spanning miles across. The puma radiates intensity with its back arched and poised to pounce on its unsuspecting prey below. The prey below does not even realize what will transpire as the puma knowingly licks its sharp teeth, thinking to itself, "YOU

ARE MINE!" about the little animals about to be devoured. As you watch this scene, if you will, step into the puma's body and become the puma. See through the puma's eyes, hear what the puma hears, and feel that unstoppably confident state the puma has as you completely become aware of just how easily you are going to devour your prey. To even more fully experience this confident state, let loose with a GROWWWLLL that rivals the best pumas alive. Doing this helps to associate this powerful state with the sound of the growl. After you do this exercise, you will be able to simply growl inside your mind and immediately go back into unstoppable confidence. Since I've done this exercise many times, I can growl and instantly transform internally what I see, hear, and feel, and my body language shifts into that of unstoppable confidence. To have your unstoppable confidence at will, all you will ever need to do again is to stop for a moment, close your eyes, growl (inside your mind) for a moment and become the puma.

The Power Of Anchors

There are both consciously set anchors and anchors that happen naturally in our environments. A police car's siren could be a negative anchor if you've been caught speeding a few times, because you may associate the siren with getting a ticket. If you find naturally occurring anchors that induce a negative state in you, notice them and interrupt them. When you interrupt them, you can then begin to consciously choose what emotional state you want to go in when you experience them. The key here is that you won't be acting out of habit. You'll be acting out of conscious choice, and that is very powerful.

∨ You can program yourself to have unstoppable confidence in the future. With this technique, you will have unstoppable confidence whenever you need it.

∨ The key to understanding this technique is that what you rehearse is what you get. A friend of mine into martial arts always reminds me to "train the way you fight because you will fight the way you train." This holds true as well for mental rehearsal regarding confidence. By rehearsing confidence in your mind, you will have confidence when the time comes when you need the confidence.

∨ Before you do anything else, stop rehearsing past incidents where you lacked confidence. Doing that only reinforces what you don't want. What you focus on is what you get, and that's why people who rehearse a lack of confidence stay stuck in the non-confident cycle of having lack of confidence, reviewing lack of confidence (and thereby programming the future for lack of confidence), and having more lack of confidence. The way your unconscious mind perceives a lack of confidence as reviewed by you is, "Hey, since you're obviously focusing on this, this must mean that lack of confidence is what you want. I'll be happy to deliver." And deliver it does all too well. Eliminate those negative incidents from your mind and avoid replaying them. If you will, imagine that your mind has certain contents in it. Some contents are very useful and help you out. Other contents of your mind such as past incidents and behaviors demonstrating a lack of confidence are not. Pretend like there's a drain in your mind and this book is liquid cleaner and that you can see the cleaner draining all the negative lack-of-confidence incidents right out of your mind forever.

For you to have this unstoppable confidence in the future, you need to mentally rehearse it now. This means we are going to mentally visualize what we desire (confidence). We will watch ourselves walking, talking, and moving confidently. We will see ourselves doing things that before we did not even realize were possible for us. Some people at this point in time contest what they cannot visualize. That's nonsense. Consider the color of your front door to your home or the color of your car. As you recall this, you can become aware that you have to be making a picture in order to get the answer to the question. Perhaps you are making pictures so rapidly that you do not perceive them consciously, yet you are visualizing. Visualizing is a skill like any other that you can and will get better with as you practice.

If you think you have difficulty visualizing, pretend that you can easily visualize. One way to deal with this is to fake it until you make it. Pretend that you can visualize and as you do that, you will develop such skill in visualizing that pretty soon you'll forget that you're just pretending and you will be a great visualizer.

On your mental movie screen, make a picture of yourself behaving confidently. Notice how you exude confidence from every fiber of your being and how others can sense this confidence coming from you. As you see yourself behaving confidently, listen in to what you hear as you fully experience that ultimate state of confidence within.

To amplify your confident state, make the picture much bigger, much brighter, and much closer. Crank the sound up all the way so that you can feel the confidence throughout your entire being. Let the bass resonate all throughout your body right now. When you make these adjustments to your experience, notice how much more powerful and confident you become.

If you have difficulty visualizing, perhaps you can first hear the sounds of confidence and then begin to focus in on the picture that is associated with those sounds. This overlap of your senses will help you more easily visualize if you need to use this tip.

Do this exercise for as many times as it takes to thoroughly feel the confidence inside you. How will you know when you've done it enough? The answer is that by looking at the picture of you confident in the future, you'll automatically feel the confidence. That is how you know you have successfully completed this exercise. Your unconscious mind does not understand the difference between a scenario that is genuinely real and a scenario that is vividly imagined. For that reason, vividly imagining confidence in your future means you are literally programming yourself to have that confidence when you need it.

These are properties of a good anchor:

1. Elicits a strong emotional state.

2. It must be unique.

3. It must be repeatable.

Here is how to set yourself up to have confidence anytime:

1. Close your eyes.

2. Go back to a time in your past and watch yourself on your mental movie screen being confident.

3. Enhance the visual and sound qualities of the movie

4. Jump into the picture as you see through your own eyes, hear what you hear, and feel that total confidence.

5. Hold your thumb and first finger together as you experience confidence.

6. The more you feel confident, the harder you press your thumb and first finger together.

7. After five seconds, separate your thumb and first finger and open your eyes.

8. Do the same thing only watching a different confident memory.

After your confidence trigger (i.e., anchor) is set, summon confidence at will by:

1. Closing your eyes.

2. Pressing your thumb and forefinger together long enough to let your confidence come flooding through you.

Circle Of Confidence

The next technique is an advanced form of anchoring called the Circle of Confidence. Instead of anchoring something to a location on your body or a to an internal thought, this technique anchors confidence to a spot on the ground. In doing this exercise, you will physically *step into confidence* whenever you need that unstoppable confidence.

There have been times in your past when you were confident. In the future, you will be confident again. The key is to be able to summon the confidence you need at will. This technique allows you to invoke a state of confidence whenever you want.

To form your circle of confidence, imagine a circular location on the floor. As you are imagining this circle, picture what it really looks like and exactly how big it is. The more vivid you can make this circle in your imagination, the more effective this exercise will be. This circle of confidence will cause you to relive your past confident experiences. Before you step into the circle, notice the following: the size of the circle, the color of the circle, or the transparency of the circle.

When you physically step into the circle, you will move back to a previous time in which you had complete confidence. Pick an experience of ultimate confidence. While you are standing in your circle of confidence, fully relive that instance of confidence. See what you saw, hear what you heard, and allow yourself to feel the ultimate confidence of that experience.

Being inside the circle of confidence and feeling confident, adjust your body language to match your confident state. Keep this confident state with you as you walk around outside the circle. If you have enough confidence to meet your outcome, you are done with the exercise. If you need more, go back into your circle of confidence and relive a different and yet equally powerful confident experience. Continue stacking up your confidence until you have all you need to get your outcome.

Regardless of wherever you are, you can use your circle of confidence to instantly gain more confidence. Exaggerate your strong, powerful physiology as you train your body how to stand and move. Pretty soon, you will find yourself naturally standing confidently as a habit.

As a bonus, realize that your circle could be a circle of any resource you need. All you need to do is go back into your past and summon the resource for your use in the present. After all, you have all the resources you need to do whatever you choose in life. It's just a matter of getting a hold of the appropriate resource at the right time.

Mirror Those Affirmations

Typically, when people do affirmations they repeat them endlessly to themselves in hope that they work. This has a degree of effectiveness, yet can be made much more effective with some modifications to how the affirmations are delivered. This technique has been modified to supercharge the efficacy of the affirmations.

Instead of using statements beginning with "I," you will use statements beginning with "You." Statements with "You" are more powerful because it's your conscious mind telling "You" [your unconscious mind] about what specifically you want and how to behave.

Get in front of a mirror and stand with confident physiology and with a mental intention to project these affirmations to change your life. The larger the mirror, the better it is so that you can see more of yourself. With your shoulders back, head held high, stomach tucked in, look squarely at yourself in the eyes and say, "You are completely powerful. You are unstoppably confident. You are becoming more and more confident each and every day. Nothing can stop you. You go for what you want congruently and powerfully. You reach your goals naturally and easily." Repeat these affirmations to yourself in the mirror until you can totally feel it in your body. You might get a different feeling. Perhaps you'll see yourself a bit differently as if you already noticed yourself having more confidence. Or potentially you'll hear your inner voice speaking more forcefully with absolute confidence within. Do this daily as part of your confidence-building regimen, and I can guarantee that you will have unstoppable confidence in little time.

The Mirror Technique exercise summary:

1. Stand in front of the mirror.

2. Adopt confident physiology (shoulders back, head up, stomach tucked in).

3. Deliver affirmations to yourself in the mirror.

4. Continue to do this each day.

Future Success Now!

If you were to taste your future success and feel what it will be like for you to be victorious when you achieve your goals, would you feel tremendously more motivated to go for it right now? This Future Succes Now! technique does exactly that. It brings all the future feelings of success into your heart, mind, and soul right now for you to experience an overwhelming sense of success so you will surrender to your passion and go for it. Any fear you may have had might still be present, but with your desire for success dominating all of your other emotions, you will take action to fulfill your goals.

In this exercise, set a strong, directed outcome that you want, and increase your confidence by doing this exercise. This means saying either out loud or inside your mind, "I'm doing this exercise to increase my confidence and feel more passion, which will naturally cause me to go after all my goals and make my dreams a reality." Read through the directions and then do the exercise. Close your eyes and picture your mental movie screen and as you are there, see yourself at the point where you are about to reach the pinnacle of your success. While you are watching yourself, make sure that you see yourself in color on a big, bright, and close picture. Fill your mind with stereo-surround sound and turn the volume up all the way. Just before you reach the pivotal point where all your success is yours, stop the movie you're watching. Ask yourself some questions to clarify why exactly you are going after this success. What is important to you about this success? What is important to you about getting this pleasure? What is important to you about that? Ultimately, what does having this success do for you?

Now restart the movie and witness yourself achieving your goal and getting all the massive success and pleasure you deserve that comes with it. Right as you fully see yourself on screen fulfilling your goal and experiencing that wonderful feeling of victory, jump into your body. See through your own eyes as if you are there now, because in your mind you are. Hear through your ears the sounds of success. Feel through every fiber of your being what success feels like. As those feelings climax, I want you to take all these wonderful feelings you have and wrap them up. Take those unlimited wonderful feelings with you as you jump out of the mental screen back into your present body as you allow all those wonderful feelings to ebb and flow throughout your body the way they were meant to do. You've smelled the sweet smell of your future success. You've tasted the victory. You realize the glory is yours for the taking. It's up to you to take action now and claim what is rightfully yours. As you complete this exercise, write down some immediate actions you will take that will bring you one step closer to achieving the success that you deserve.

Here is the Future Success Now! exercise summary:

1. Close your eyes and play a movie on your mental movie screen of you massively succeeding.

2. Just at the point when you are about to get to the peak of your success in the movie, stop the movie temporarily.

3. Ask yourself, "What's important to me about this success? What will having this success do for me? What does this success mean to me?"

4. Jump into the movie as you begin playing it again. See through your eyes as you succeed. Hear through your own ears as you succeed. Feel what it's like for you to soak up the unlimited, massive success you know you deserve.

5. When the movie is done, take all of these wonderful feelings back to you and open your eyes.

6. Write down five immediate actions you will take that will bring you one step closer to achieving your goals.

Put Your Life In Perspective

Consider the event or person or whatever that might appear overwhelming to you now and that you may fear. Notice what it's like to you. By the end of the exercise, you will think about it completely differently and have much more confidence about what you're going to do.

Picture a line of time representing your lifetime. Represent your past off to the left, your present in the center, and your future off to the right. Now place whatever was bothering you on the timeline and visualize it as a small dot. With this small dot on your timeline, mentally step back so you can see a larger portion of your entire timeline instead of just the present. Notice how already this puts that minor nuisance into a different perspective? Now, mentally step back even further to notice all of your past and all of your future at once and recognize just how small and insignificant this dot representing your current problem is.

When you keep things in perspective, it's really difficult to waste valuable time and energy on trivial things. That tiny issue that used to be a problem no longer is when you keep the big picture in view. The trouble begins when people do not keep the big picture in sight and magnify the little issue to be larger than it really is.

Here is the Life in Perspective technique summary:

1. Imagine a line of time representing your life, with your past coming from the left and the future going toward the right.

2. Notice the small event, which you "fear," and how small it is relative to your entire life's timeline.

3. Now zoom out from your timeline and notice how the timeline of all of time can come into picture now, with the entire past history of the universe coming from the left and the entire future of the universe stretching to the far right. The center of the timeline is the present time.

4. Notice how your small event that you used to fear is small in comparison to your life and notice how small your life timeline is in comparison to the span of the universe.

5. Zoom in and out to understand the relative importance of this event and keep things really in perspective, where they belong.

Looking And Chatting With Your Future

People are motivated either by moving toward pleasure or by moving away ✓ from pain. If we were bunny rabbits, it would be equivalent to us moving toward carrots or away from boots. This next technique will work best on people who move away from pain, because it amplifies the pain of not going after your dreams to the point where it's easier to just go fulfill your dreams than experience the pain of not doing it.

Read through all of these instructions and then do them. Close your eyes and imagine a line of your time representing your past, present, and future off to the left, center, and right, respectively. Imagine floating up above your timeline and drifting forward far into your future. Continue floating forward in time until you go to the point right before the end of your life. As you get to that point, see yourself on your mental movie screen lying down on your deathbed. Notice the extreme sadness in your facial expressions and the way you communicate unfulfillment with the way you move your body. In doing this, you might realize that you are looking at a person who has lived a life unfulfilled. Tune in to the sounds that are coming from that old person who had so much potential in their lives yet somehow failed to take action and live their dreams. Make the picture that you are watching very big, very bright, and very close. Just as the feeling rises of extreme disappointment as your future self realizes a life has not been invested wisely, jump right into that old person's body and see what that experience is like. Hear what that experience is like and ultimately feel how awful it feels to lead a life unfulfilled.

It's really quite tragic, isn't it? When you fully experience that feeling of unful-fillment, deep regret, pain, disappointment, and frustration that you WILL feel if you don't go after your dreams through immediately taking action, jump outside the mental movie screen and come back into yourself. If you don't take action immediately to go after your dreams, at the end of your life this is how you will feel. Since you've experienced the pain that will happen if you don't go after it right now, are you aware of how much more motivated you are to avoid that feeling and live your dreams? If you hesitate in the future, call up that horrible feeling from this experience and allow that to propel you to take action now. To break out of the negative state of mind induced by the past exercise, name three different objects in the room and then physically move to a different location to get into a better state.

Instead of ending up in a neutral state, now visualize yourself with your ideal future. See, hear, and feel what you will experience when you are leading your dream life. Use the techniques that you have learned in this book to fully bring your ideal future to life. Fully step into that world that will be yours in the future. Discover just how motivated you can become when you visualize that perfect future of yours.

Build An Enriched Past

Many times a lack of confidence stems from not having done something before. And in order to get good at doing something, usually you have to do it poorly at first. Doing something poorly at first causes people anxiety and a lack of confidence, since sometimes we falsely labor under the impression that we have to do everything perfectly from the start. How much more confident would you feel if you knew that you had done something many times before? I'm willing to bet you would be tremendously more confident. This next technique builds on past successes of you succeeding wildly at what it is you're about to do.

You may or may not have heard of false memory syndrome. False memory syndrome is where someone can get someone else to create false memories of events that didn't really happen. However, the false memories are so vividly imagined that they appear to be very real and, consequently, people act as if they are. Sometimes people implant disempowering false memories into one another. What if we were to create false memories of our own past having massive success at what we're really only going to do for the first time? How much more confidence will you have when you do this?

Build into your past as many successes as you find necessary. You will do this by really visualizing success at what you're about to do and imagining it as if it happened in the past. As you create your past successes, really intensify the experience so that you catch the feeling of confidence and success you need.

Here is the Enriched Past Technique summary:

1. See yourself in your past, on your mental movie screen, doing what you are actually about to do for the first time, massively succeeding.

2. Crank up all the visual and sound qualities to make the new "memory" really intense and real.

3. Do this ten times to create ten different positive "memories" of your success.

When I was starting out in public speaking, I had no experience at all, and since I needed to rapidly gain experience to be credible, I went back into my past and created an entire series of memories. Even though I consciously knew they were false memories, they were so vividly imagined that my unconscious mind knew no difference and consequently allowed me to behave as if I had been speaking a lot. I imagined that I had an entire history of making wonderful speeches, motivating audiences, and receiving standing ovations for my abilities. To go one step further, I imagined people taking my message to heart, acting on it, and transforming their lives. By creating all of these memories, by the time I got up to actually speak for the first time it was delightfully simple and I radiated confidence from the beginning. Anyone can use these techniques to better themselves. It's just a matter of knowing the techniques and applying them to your life.

Correct Past Mistakes

With the last technique, we created imaginary past successes to help us be confident in the future. It made it easier for us to act as if we had already done what in reality we were doing for the first time. This next technique goes into the past and corrects past mistakes in a similar fashion.

Go back to a time when you really blew it. Perhaps you didn't go for it as you should or something was not the smashing success you intended it to be. Close your eyes and watch yourself on the mental movie screen as you rerun the movie of you just about to make the mistake or screw things up. Just prior to the instant in time when you're about to start deviating from your success path and start making mistakes, stop the movie. We stop the movie now because we don't want you rehearsing the negative incident, for that only reinforces it as a way of behaving. While the movie is stopped, think about how the situation ideally would have turned out if you could make any ending to this personal movie. Restart the movie and replace the old ending with the ideal ending. See, hear, and feel yourself succeeding the way in which you deserve. Now run the entire movie from start to finish with the ideal solution ten times. What this does is recode the past incident as a success to the mind. Furthermore, it teaches the mind to create success in the future, because we have rehearsed and reinforced that success. After you've watched the movie from start to finish from a third person point of view, jump into the movie and run it from start to finish with the ideal solution as you see through your eyes, hear what you hear, and feel that massive success that is yours. Rerun the movie with you in it ten times.

Now as you look back onto your past, you'll notice how things feel differently. Your past has been enriched and you'll discover yourself moving through the world more resourcefully. One neat thing about this technique is the versatility: you can correct all parts of your past with whatever you want.

Here is the Mistakes To Successes technique summary:

1. Watch yourself in the past on your mental movie screen right up to the point where you would have made the mistake.

2. At that point, stop the movie and think about the resource you need to add and the ideal finish to this movie is.

3. Finish the movie with the ideal solution, you behaving resourcefully and getting your outcome.

4. Jump inside the beginning of the movie and let it run from start to finish with the ideal solution, seeing what you see, hearing what you hear, and feeling what it's like to get your outcome.

5. Run the movie of the success ten times to lock it in.

The Domino Effect

As you recall from earlier in the book, beliefs come in two different forms: causality and meaning. The causality form of belief is "X causes Y" or "Y happens because of X." The meaning form of beliefs is "X is Y" or "X means Y." Understanding how beliefs are structured means we can consciously choose those beliefs that are most empowering to us. For example, if someone believes "Public speaking means it's time to be fearful and lack confidence," then obviously that person's behavior will manifest what they believe as they consequently get nervous before making a speech. It's necessary to understand how beliefs are formed for use in this next technique.

Think of something that is so far outside your comfort zone that you would be absolutely amazed, surprised, and delighted if you actually did it. In thinking about this, keep in mind that it should be something that is feasible and something that you could immediately do should you make that decision to take action. Become aware of what specifically you would see, hear, and feel when doing it. Now ponder what sort of confidence it would take for you to do that.

When you've thought of something completely outside your comfort zone, you naturally realize that if you do this, you can do anything you want to do in the world. After all, if you can step so far outside your comfort zone by doing this, you can continue to expand your comfort zone by stepping outside it, can't you? To make this exercise really work well, lock in the belief in your heart, mind, and spirit that doing whatever it is you are thinking of right now that is far outside your comfort zone means that you can do anything you want to do in life.

I chose skydiving as my activity that was far outside my comfort zone. I had never done anything so daring and had led a pretty conservative lifestyle and always minimized all risks. Some risks are good to take and some risks should be avoided. To gain more confidence in myself, I built in the belief that "As I jump out of an airplane and hurtle to the ground at rapid speeds, I will be stepping far outside my comfort zone. And by proving to myself that I can step outside my comfort zone to do things I wasn't quite sure I could do, that means I know I can do anything in this world." Skydiving for me demonstrated that anything is possible for me in this world. When you do your activity, you'll realize that anything is possible for you in this world.

Your example can be whatever you want it to be as long as it is a far stretch outside your comfort zone. It could be marching into your boss's office and asking for a raise, speaking in public, or training for and running a marathon. The most important part is that when you make it happen, you will realize that anything is possible for you when you set your mind to it.

When you've decided what you're going to do, take immediate action to ensure that it will happen. Get things in motion as soon as you can. Taking immediate action is an excellent habit to develop. The most successful, unstoppably confident people take immediate action and accordingly manifest their dreams sooner.

For anyone who is very logically or critically oriented, the belief that "Since I can skydive, I can do anything" is not very logical at all. Yet, holding the belief that "I can do anything" will enable you to go for much, much more than someone who has limited themselves with "logic." You may not be able to do "anything," but you will definitely go past your old limits. Remember, what seems like a limit is very often just a limit in *belief*, not reality. When you choose your new beliefs, choose them because they are useful and empowering, not from so-called logic. Choose your new beliefs because they serve *you* in living your dreams.

Here is a Domino Effect exercise summary:

1. Think of a feasible and yet most extraordinary thing you can do that is outside your comfort zone.

2. Build in the belief that if you do this extraordinary thing it means that you can do anything you want to in this world.

3. Do the extraordinary thing you chose in step one. Congratulations! You can now do anything you want in this world!

Borrow Confidence From Someone Else

A great way to gain confidence is to model someone else who already has a lot of confidence. If you use this technique to enhance your confidence in your career, your mentor or someone really experienced at what you do with a lot of confidence will make a great model. Anyone who has an absolute belief in himself will make a good model for you. One way to supercharge your results using this technique is to repeat this technique with several different models of unstoppable confidence.

Once you've identified the person who embodies confidence to you, you want to get to know, as thoroughly as possible, how they move through the world. To do this, spend as much time as you can with them and talk with them about how they think about confidence, life, and going for it. If your model of confidence is not accessible to you, perhaps you can get to know the person vicariously by purchasing their books, CDs, or home-study courses, or by attending their seminars. If it's a rock star, you could go to their concert. If it's a star athlete, perhaps you could attend their sporting event. The idea here is to expose your mind to them as much as possible. The better grasp you have on their beliefs, attitudes, and values, the more effective you can model their confidence.

Set a strong outcome for this exercise, such as, "I want confidence from [name your model of confidence] for these reasons…[list reasons]." Read through these directions and then perform the technique. By the time you reach this point, you have already familiarized yourself with your model of confidence and have a good grasp on how they perceive the world and their belief in themselves and what they do.

Close your eyes and see a movie of your model of confidence being unstoppably confident. Pay close attention to how they speak, move, gesture, and walk. Become aware of how they interact with others. Imagine how they talk to themselves internally, how they carry themselves, and anything else you can notice about them. Make the movie very big, very bright, and very close. Turn the sounds of the movie up all the way so that it resonates in you.

Next, step into the movie as if you are stepping into your confidence model's body. Take on their entire being. See as if you are seeing through their eyes, hearing with their ears, and feeling what it is like to completely immerse yourself and be as unstoppably confident as them. While you are "inside them," physically do all you can to be like them. Gesture, speak, move, walk, and have the same facial expressions as them. Continue doing this until you fully understand what it feels like to be them, with unstoppable confidence.

If it helps, imagine yourself as them in different contexts. When you fully have that unstoppable confidence, see yourself stepping outside their body and back into your own. As you float back into your own body, take with you that unstoppably confident feeling you've just created. Integrate that feeling into your body, your mind, and your identity. By having this unstoppable confidence once means you can have it any time you want simply by doing this exercise. After you do this exercise a number of times, your unstoppable confidence habit will begin and you will have confidence naturally without having to perform this technique each time.

Here's the Borrowed Confidence technique summary:

1. Find someone whose confidence you'd like to have for yourself.

2. Expose yourself to that model of confidence as much as possible. Chat with them if possible, read their books, listen to their CDs, watch their movies, attend their concerts, etc.

3. Watch your role model behaving confidently on your mental movie screen. Notice how they move through the world, how they speak and gesture.

4. Make the image really compelling by turning up the visual, sound, and feeling qualities of the movie.

5. Step into the movie and become the model. See through the confidence model's eyes, hear what they hear, feel what they feel. Gesture, speak, and move through the world as they do with this unstoppable confidence.

6. Step into the model during five different instances when the model is absolutely confident. This allows you to understand how they have their confidence.

7. When you feel you have a handle on how they have their confidence, step outside the model body, take what you learned about how to be confident, and integrate them back into yourself.

Schedule Your Dreams

Successful people plan their work and then work their plan. This technique will help you decide what you want and focus your energy to pursuing it. Goals are dreams with deadlines. For that reason, this technique gives you some specific deadlines for when you want to achieve your dreams.

What I want you to do is give yourself permission to dream and play like a child for a moment. Imagine yourself five years into the future living your ideal lifestyle. What sort of job do you have? What have you accomplished? Where do you live? What is your lifestyle like? Focus in on the answers to these questions.

With the answers to these questions, build what I call an expanded resume. A typical resume presents your to your employer in order to get yourself hired. It charts what you have accomplished and the skills you possess now. The expanded resume encompasses your entire life: your family life, your career, your social circle, your spirituality, your finances, etc. Create this resume that will be true for you in five years. Be sure to stretch yourself, because stretching ourselves is what causes us to grow and develop as people. Reread this resume once a week or more often if you can invest the time, and in five years time, you will have accomplished much if not all of what you put down.

A similar technique for channeling your energy into the direction you want is to construct a future magazine cover with you on it. The magazine could be either a real or fictitious magazine that shows you succeeding in whatever area of life you choose. When I did this, I used computer presentation software to import my photograph, design the magazine cover, and place catchy head-lines for the front cover that described what I will achieve. When the cover was finished, I printed it out and proudly displayed it on my desk. From time to time, I glance over at my desk to find it there and automatically become more motivated to take action to move toward my goals.

Focus Outward For More Confidence

People who are shy and people who are confident place their attention in different places. Shy people tend to focus inward by constantly analyzing their last statements and how people perceive it, and they eavesdrop on their endless internal chatter while trying to maintain a conversation. Confident people place their attention on the person or people to whom they are speaking. One hundred percent of their focus is there, and they trust them-selves to adjust their communication automatically based upon the feed-back that they get from their conversation partner or partners.

Public speaking is a perfect example of this. Excellent speakers set an out-come to motivate people, practice their material well, and then get up there and go for it. They pay attention to how the audience is reacting and adjust accordingly. This is what makes their speeches so powerful. They care if their message is getting through to the audience. Speakers who are less experienced and shy split their attention between their internal dialogue and the audience. They are doing their best to deliver the speech at the same time they hear "I am not confident. Is my zipper unzipped? Are they staring at me for some other reason than why I'm speaking? Do I have food caught in my teeth? How long until this is over?" This divided attention deprives the audience of what could be a great speech. Instead, the audi-ence suffers through a mediocre speech in which the speaker is too blind to watch the feedback the audience is giving because the speaker's inter-nal dialogue gets the higher priority. There is only a certain amount of con-scious attention that we can direct. It is best to direct it to the person or people to whom we are speaking with.

If you find yourself going inside to have an internal chat, stop yourself and come back out. Promise that you'll chat with yourself later on. People will notice the difference when you are entirely with them or when you're having two conversations: one with them and one with yourself. Remember to con-sistently focus your attention outward for the best possible communication. I'm sure you appreciate it when people give you their full attention when they communicate with you, and you know they'll appreciate it as much as you do when you put your focus on them.

Teaching Unstoppable Confidence To Others

To teach unstoppable confidence to others and to increase your own confidence, I recommend meeting regularly with other like-minded people for the express purpose of developing your confidence. Let this book serve as a guide while your group does the confidence exercises. Getting together with like-minded people is incredibly powerful. They can support you and you can support them on your journey to greater success. When you get together with others, you can talk about situations where you were confident and situations where you needed more confidence. They may have insights for you on your situation that haven't occurred to you. Meet with these people on a regular basis. Once a month would be great. Harness the power of synergy. Synergy, if you're not familiar with it, is the concept that the whole is greater than the sum of the parts. In the case of your confidence group, the entire group's intelligence exceeds that of each individual's intelligence summed up.

Teach these skills to everyone you know, especially kids. You are never too young or too old to benefit from these skills. Imagine what your life would be like right now if you had learned these skills as a youth. You can make that happen for any children in your life.

Swish Into Confidence

The next technique is called the "swish" technique, because you redirect your brain as rapidly as you can make the "swish" sound. The specific instructions for how to do the technique will be given a bit later.

Our minds are trained to go in a certain direction. They are encoded to pursue pleasure and avoid pain. Sometimes, if we have not been consciously directing our minds, our minds gravitate toward less than resourceful behaviors. One of these behaviors is shyness. This pattern redirects the brain by saying to the mind, "Not shy, confident!"

If you act shy, you do it out of a pattern you've either consciously or unconsciously set up for yourself. There are triggers as to when to begin the shy pattern. For you, sometimes you get a cue to begin acting shy. What we're going to do is take that same cue and retrain you to be cued to be confident, instead.

Think of a time when you act shy. Decide on what the initial cue is that lets you know it's time to be shy. For some people, arriving at a party full of strangers and looking at their foreign faces is a cue to begin acting shy. For others, seeing an attractive member of the opposite sex sit down nearby is their cue to act shy. Find out what your cue is. People do not randomly become shy. There is always a cue that precedes it.

For this technique, it's useful to understand a few terms. *Associated* means you're looking through your own eyes, hearing with your own ears, and feeling whatever is in your body. *Dissociated* means that you are looking at yourself from a third-person perspective as if you're watching yourself on a mental movie screen.

Now that you've discovered the cue that has lead to unresourceful states, experience that cue from an associated (first-person) position. Practice making the picture of what you see smaller, darker, and farther away. Take the normal picture and make it small, dark, and really far away as fast as you can say out loud, "Swish!" Do this enough times until you feel you can make the picture of when you're about to be shy disappear very quickly.

Following that, picture a dissociated (third person perspective) image of your ideal self. Picture yourself and how you want to behave instead of how you currently do. See strong, confident body language, facial expressions, and gestures, and make sure that when you think about your ideal self, you feel really motivated to be that way. If you don't feel a strong sense of motivation, adjust the image of your ideal self until you do. Make this picture small, dark, and far away at first, and practice making this picture really big, really bright, and really close as rapidly as you can say out loud, "Swish!" Practice this enough times until you can do it easily.

Now what we're going to do is retrain your mind so that whenever it experiences the cue image, it will automatically flash to the ideal self and therefore draw you into being your ideal self. When you've done this successfully, you will see the trigger that used to make you shy and immediately experience an unconscious shift to more confidence.

Close your eyes and see the cue image in the forefront of your mind. See it big, bright, and close up, just like you would if you were experiencing it for real. In the lower right hand corner, see the ideal self-image as smaller, darker, and farther away. While you make the "swish" sound, immediately flip the two pictures so the cue image becomes small, dark, and far away, and disappears as the ideal self image becomes really big, really bright, and really close. Make the "swish" sound as you do this exercise because it will help you unconsciously move the pictures around.

Pause for a moment, open your eyes to clear your mind, and then reset the pictures so you see the cue image big and close and your confident self in the lower right-hand corner. Then make the "swish" sound as you transpose them in the same way you did previously. Continue to repeat this pausing, resetting, and "swishing" of pictures until you can simply look at the cue image and your brain automatically gravitates toward the ideal self-image. That's how you know you've been successful in retraining your mind.

Dissociate — Add Resources — Act Differently

Many times people are overwhelmed by something due to the fact that they are too close to the situation. If someone is too close to the situation, it may be difficult for them to reason logically. For example, if you have to make a major decision and there is an overriding emotional component, that emotional component may skew your judgment. This technique helps you stand back and survey the big picture in order to make the best decision for yourself.

What you will do in this technique is observe yourself with a third-person point of view. That means that you will step outside your body and look over at yourself making a decision. To do this, picture yourself on a mental movie screen in the same situation, except you are now a detached observer. Pretend that you are the narrator as you refer to yourself in the third person. Refer to yourself in third-person by repeatedly using your name. Think through the process out loud in a third-person, detached frame of mind. As your narrate your thinking process regarding the decision, be sure you have confident physiology and tonality. This will help you make a firm commitment to the ultimate decision you arrive at. Your decisions will be more rational as a result of this, and emotion will influence your decisions less since you literally have some distance from the situation.

Another way to think about this is to think about having a chat with a clone of yourself and going over the situation, bouncing ideas back and forth between one another, before fully deciding what you want to do. Remember that you are the adviser doling out advice to your clone, and not the seeker of advice in this particular instance. Give your clone the advice you naturally feel you would. That advice is what you truly ought to do.

The Confidence Resource Triangle

The confidence resource triangle uses the same principles as the Dissociate — Add Resources technique described previously. The main difference is that it uses physical locations to represent the different states.

The Confidence Resource Triangle has three legs to it: a stuck state location, a dissociated "observer" location, and a resource location. The *stuck state* is the state where one will experience what it's like to be stuck in a particular situation and need a resource. The *dissociated location* is the location where a person can stand back and objectively look at the stuck situation from a third person point of view. The *resource location* is the location that represents a resource that would get a person unstuck when added to the stuck state.

Label three different spots on the floor as "S" for stuck, "D" for dissociated and "R" for resource. It helps to have the labels when you first do this exercise. Later on, you will be able to simply mentally mark out locations on the floor that represent the different ideas.

First, step onto the stuck location. The stuck location should be a context in your mind where you need more confidence. Close your eyes if it helps you. See what you see in that situation. Hear what you hear when you need more confidence. Feel what it feels like to need more confidence. Just when you've gotten a taste of it, step outside the location. Name three different things in the room to break your state and thus get you out of your stuck state.

Second, step onto the dissociated location. See the same context where you were stuck and needed confidence, only now see it from a third-person perspective. Notice how it's different, and you can perceive things more objectively. Think of a confidence resource that would be useful for you to have to conquer this stuck state.

Third, step onto the resource location. As you step onto the resource location, step into the resource by completely reliving past times when you were confident. See what you saw, hear what you heard, and feel what it's like to really crank up your confidence level right now. You can think of this resource location as a miniature circle of confidence.

Now, with this overwhelming confidence, take this confidence and step back into what was the stuck state. Notice how things are changed as you have infinitely more confidence. How do you act differently with so much more confidence? How easily and naturally do you get unstuck with all this confidence oozing from every fiber of your being?

If for some reason your stuck state did not change for you as much as you liked, do the exercise again and continue stacking up confident resources and bringing them to the stuck state until things change.

Again, this can be used for any resource and any stuck state. The only limits are your imagination. Since this is a book about confidence, however, the example demonstrates a confidence resource state.

Your Confident Clone

Imagine that you could clone yourself and everything about you would be the same, except your new clone would have infinitely more confidence than you do presently. Short of being able to do that and send your clone off to fulfill your dreams by taking action, there is this technique. Just suppose there is a confident clone of you. Watch how he or she walks, talks, speaks, gestures, and moves in general. Really notice it.

Sneak up behind your clone. At the back of your confident clone, you'll notice a zipper running from the top of its head down to the bottom of its back. Unzip the zipper and step into your confident clone's body. See through his eyes. Hear through his ears. Feel what it's like to project unlimited confidence. Begin to move, speak, gesture, and walk like your confident clone. Remember that this is make-believe and you can pretend anything and master it. You'll note that this is a derivation of the technique of borrowing from someone else, yet now you're borrowing from your confident self.

If you forget to step back into a lesser confident you while you're in your confident clone, that's just fine. You'll just have to go on being even more confident than before. If you keep it up, pretty soon you'll forget that you're pretending and you'll naturally be unstoppably confident!

> You have all the resources within you to be, do,
> and have anything you want in this world.
>
> — Kent Sayre

your
confident future

Whatever we expect with confidence becomes
our own self-fulfilling prophecy.
— Brian Tracy

Masters are masters because they make more mistakes. The more mistakes one makes, the more distinctions they'll get. The more distinctions one has, the more easily they will reach their outcome later on. Think about that as it applies to your confidence and going after your dreams. Masters are excellent at the fundamentals. They go back and ensure they have gotten the basics down. If for some reason in the future you hit a confidence roadblock, come back to this book and use it as your reference.

Confidence And Taking Action Now

The point of power is in the present. That means we need to end the procrastination and *do it now*. I cannot emphasize this attitude strongly enough. Dismiss the "That can wait until later" mentality. The sooner you adopt the do-it-now mentality, the sooner you will create better relationships, have more fun in life, and fulfill your dreams.

The reason doing things right now as soon as you possibly can is easier than procrastinating is because of the psychic wait. If you procrastinate on something, you might typically think to yourself, "I should be doing that instead of this." Then you might talk yourself into doing it later. Meanwhile, the leisure activity, which you were supposed to be enjoying, is now consequently ruined due to the fact that your mind is preoccupied with what you should be doing. Or worse yet, you might be feeling guilty for not doing what you should do. This procrastination attitude ruins your leisure and does not get things done. That is why the do-it-now mentality is so powerful. When you get it down to where it is a habit, it's really much easier to set up tasks and get them done and then, free from anything else on your mind as a result of taking care of your obligations, you can enjoy yourself in your favorite leisure activity.

The great equalizer amongst us all is that we all have twenty-four hours in each and every day to invest. It's too bad yet, most people don't think of their time as an investment. Once you've spent today's twenty-four hours, you can NEVER get them back. EVER. People dawdle or endlessly hang out without realizing that time can never be recaptured. I'm all for leisure and spending quality time with friends and loved ones. That's a great way to spend one's time. My main objection is people acting without purpose. Or, rather, being inactive without purpose. If people consciously choose to spend their time, that is great. It's when they are just drifting along without any respect to time that it becomes a problem.

To maximize the use of your time, survey your life. Find what wastes your time and eliminate it. Find what you thoroughly enjoy and spend more time doing that. No matter what it is, increase your time invested in that activity. If something is unbearable to you, hire it out. Or perhaps trade responsibilities with a friend, partner, or spouse. Do more of what you like and less of what you don't.

The following is an exercise to discover how you invest your time. When you get done with it, the results might surprise you. Go through your results and eliminate the time wasters. Maximize doing what you love. You will discover that you're more efficient the weeks thereafter since you will know what tasks consume large chunks of your time and what tasks can be delegated.

Discovering How You Invest Your Time exercise summary:

1. For an entire week, write down what you are doing every half hour.

2. At the end of the week, notice where you spend most of your time.

3. Ask yourself how easily and naturally you can eliminate time-wasting activities.

4. Ask yourself how you can invest more time in the activities that will lead you closer to your goals.

5. Schedule your next week according to what you discover.

As you continue to use your time ever more wisely and productively, notice how this increases your confidence. The more actions you take to use your time wisely and make your dreams and wishes come true, the more motivated you will feel to do and achieve even more. The proper fruit of knowledge is action. Take action and reap the full benefits of your knowledge.

Staying On Track With Your Confidence Practice Calendar

One method to stay on track as you develop your ability to be confident at will is to buy a calendar and make it your confidence practice calendar. You can take an ordinary calendar and schedule which confidence exercises you do on which particular days. Furthermore, you can set up confidence milestones that you expect to achieve on your journey toward unlimited confidence.

One day you could practice speaking confidently. The next day, the day's exercise could be walking confidently. The following day's exercise could be gesturing confidently. Go through this book and pick out your favorite exercises and put them down on your calendar. Create the calendar to best match your personality. You will know what will work best for you.

You will get more of what you reinforce. Therefore, I recommend that you praise yourself when you find yourself behaving confidently. Although you might think it's a bit corny (I know I did when I first did it), I found that the following method really works as a method of reinforcement. When I found myself behaving in a way that I wanted, I gave myself a small round of applause, a pat on the back, and a self-hug. Many people deny themselves their due credit even when they perform extraordinarily. Give yourself credit by consciously reinforcing your positive behavior.

After all, who is the only person you are guaranteed to be with for twenty-four hours every day for the rest of your life? You are, of course. Treat yourself well and discover how your unconscious mind will respond to you. As you treat yourself better and better, you'll discover that you're better able to access parts of your memory that you hadn't before, you'll be able to visualize better, and that your negative internal dialogue will disappear.

Many people do not treat themselves very well. They have a constant, nagging internal dialogue making their lives miserable. They come from a frame of mind of scarcity and that people are out to get them. People are causes in their lives, not effects. Disempowered people let things happen to them. Empowered people make things happen in their lives. That means that when a person takes complete responsibility over their entire lives, they begin to become very empowered. They realize they always have a choice and act out of conscious choice instead of blaming or playing the victim role.

When you are empowered and act out of choice, celebrate your accomplishments by rewarding yourself. Reward yourself in the same way that you'd reward your best friend for his or her accomplishments. After all, who better to have as a best friend than yourself? Remind yourself that you are wonderful. Sometimes people don't celebrate their accomplishments. They stall or wait for others to do it. Maybe they want permission to celebrate what they did. I'm now giving my permission for you to celebrate all of your successes.

You can have it all. Just like Napoleon Hill said, "If you can conceive it, you can believe it, then you can achieve it." And that's an absolute truth.

Three Key Components For Healthy Living

Flexibility

There are three components that are essential to leading a healthy, fulfilling life: flexibility, a sense of humor, and an orientation toward the future. Flexibility means that you have enough choices to do what is most appropriate for the situation in order to achieve your outcome. If something does not work, you have the sensory acuity to realize that it's not working and adjust your behavior (i.e., have flexibility) based on that feedback until you eventually get your result. The more flexible someone is, the more likely they will get what they want. There is a law of cybernetics that states, "The person or component with the most choices in the system wins."

Take negotiation, for example. If someone has many options and the opposition has few, the first party has the upper hand. The fewer options one has, the less empowered one is. Maximize your empowerment by being flexible, by having as many options and choices that you can imagine.

Sense Of Humor

Having a sense of humor is essential in life. Having a sense of humor means you won't take things in life too seriously or blow them out of proportion. I'm sure we all know people who take things too seriously and end up having health problems and smoking and drinking to escape from their seriousness. A more useful way for to experience life is by laughing your way through it. When times are the toughest, when you are completely stressed out, when you're under a deadline, the ability to laugh out loud is truly priceless. Laughing out loud will help to center you, which will lead you into a more resourceful state for solving the problem in the forefront of your mind. People who are excessively serious and overly formal tend to get ulcers, have heart attacks, strokes, and the like, because they choose to allow themselves to get stressed out too much. It's true that people who laugh are healthier and live longer; keep your sense of humor as you go through your journey.

Future Orientation

There are three different ways we can orient ourselves with respect to time: to the past, to the present, and to the future. They each can be useful in their own contexts, yet having a strong future orientation is the best for living your dream life.

A past orientation can be useful for summoning positive resources from your past. Some people who are strictly oriented toward the past virtually live in the past by always rehashing the past through story telling and other reminiscing. Focusing solely on the past will cause people to fail to take action to build their futures.

The ideal orientation is to balance the future and present orientations. People who get overly caught up in a present time orientation live entirely in the moment while they fail to plan for the future. This flawed orientation begets dire consequences. They want immediate gratification without always thinking about the negative effects of their decisions. A certain amount of present time orientation is great for cherishing each and every moment of your life and allowing for spontaneity, provided that you still plan for the future.

Knowing what you want for the future, planning for it, and taking action while enjoying yourself in the present moment is the ultimate ideal to strive for. By delaying instant gratification, having patience, and diligently working toward your goals as you thrive on each small step toward fulfilling your dreams, you will have the ideal present and future time orientation combination. When you find the balance that works best for you, you'll know it.

Whose Limits Are These?

Remember, anybody who tells you that something can't be done really means that they can't do it or don't know anyone who can. They are talking about their own perceived limits. Remember that.

Thomas Edison did more than ten thousand experiments before he perfected the incandescent light bulb. Colonel Sanders, the founder of chicken franchise KFC, got one thousand and nine rejections before someone bought his chicken recipe. When Sylvester Stallone of *Rambo* fame showed up to Hollywood, he went through over a hundred auditions before someone cast him in a small role.

What all of these people had in common was that they realized there is no such thing as failure, there are only results. After you've been knocked down, the only thing that matters is that you get back up.

As Thomas Edison was developing the light bulb, a newspaper reporter came to interview him about his experiments that had "failed." The newspaper reporter inquired as to when the inventor would ever give up after failing over ten thousand times, to which Edison retorted, "Never." The pressing newspaper reporter insisted, "But you keep failing over and over." Edison swiftly responded, "No, what you don't understand is that I haven't failed. I've just found over ten thousand ways not to invent the light bulb." This is very true since he learned and corrected from each previous experiment. It's the whole idea of failing forward. My personal motto is to *Fail forward fast*. The faster you do this, the sooner you learn from your mistakes, which means the sooner you get the ultimate results you want.

A jet flying nonstop from Los Angeles to New York is going to be off course over ninety-five percent of the time. Five percent of the time the jet will be flying perfectly on course. The remaining amount of time that the jet is off course accounts for adjustments based on turbulence, weather, avoiding other planes, etc. The pilots thankfully don't set the jet on autopilot and then go to sleep in the cockpit. They constantly read the instrument panel for feedback and adjust accordingly. They are talking to the ground control tower that gives them feedback as well. Even though they fly "off course" for so much of the time, they always reach their end destination. Just like you will.

If at first you're not successful at a venture, be thankful. Some of the least successful people out there got an early success and decided that what they did was the ultimate and there was no room for improvement so they became complacent and stagnated. Compare this to someone else who fails royally the first few times when beginning a new venture. These late bloomers have to develop skills of how to adjust their behavior based on feedback. These late bloomers tend to develop habits to always be improving. As they develop these habits and begin to succeed, they eventually surpass the early bloomers in productivity.

Life is short and we don't know what tomorrow holds for us. We can plan for a wonderful future while we make the most of today. You can achieve your dreams when you take action and work your plan. Life goes by so quickly that we must remind ourselves to cherish each and every moment.

Avoiding Arrogance

As you will remember from the first chapter, arrogance and confidence are two entirely separate things. There are a few guidelines to follow to stay grounded while still having unstoppable confidence. When you follow these, you will assure yourself that you won't be arrogant, but will stay humble and grounded even as you grow more confident.

Have an attitude of gratitude for what you have and all your gifts in life. Begin each day thanking the universe or God for what you have and all your gifts. This will help center you and start your day off positively when you consider how much you have going for you.

Being arrogant is less effective since arrogant people rarely care what others think to the point that they disregard valuable feedback that would help them out in life. If an arrogant person does not take another person's feelings into account when talking with them, the connection between the two people will be much more shallow and thus less effective. Let yourself find the right balance of being aware of other's needs, desires, and ideas.

With your completely resourceful self, have the frame of mind to always come from a position of power and choice. Come from a position of abundance and deservedness. In every situation as you develop this habit, ask yourself, "Am I coming from a place of choice, power, abundance, and deservedness?" If so, congratulate yourself. If not, adjust your mindset accordingly. You'll get better results when you have this abundance mentality.

Prepare For Your Unstoppable Future

As your confidence in yourself grows, others will notice the change within you and perhaps behave differently than before. That's normal. They are used to you acting in a particular way and when you behave differently, they might not have a pattern for interacting with you anymore. They will adapt to your newfound confidence and develop an affinity to it. When I first began breaking out of my shy shell, I was concerned about how others would treat me. Much to my delight, they more thoroughly enjoyed being around me as a direct result of my increased confidence.

Regarding friends and family, enlist their support to help you on your confidence journey. When you are behaving in a confident manner, they can compliment you and reinforce the behavior. Take the responsibility to tell them that you would appreciate their support as you do these confidence exercises to become more and more confident. Similarly, if they catch you falling into old, unresourceful, shy habits, they can politely point that out to you, which means you can immediately correct that behavior.

Some people may have negative reactions to your enhanced confidence and zest for life. They are not your genuine friends. Your genuine friends want the best for you and anything less means they are not your true friends. Being a great friend means wanting the best for your friends at all times. If someone tries in vain to criticize your increased confidence, view this as an opportunity to be confident about your confidence and let that criticism bounce right off you without making any impact.

With your unstoppable confidence, you're going to want to tackle the world at once. You *can* tackle the world, yet do it in progressive stages. You will have so many dreams and passions awakened that it may seem overwhelming when you consider all that you want to and *can* achieve in your lifetime.

Considering everything at once is a great way to feel overwhelmed. Sometimes when people feel overwhelmed by everything, they do nothing because they don't know where to begin. Avoid this. Consider your most important, immediate goals and pursue those first. Remember to take action each and every day no matter how big or small — this brings you closer to fulfilling your goals. A journey of a thousand miles begins with a single step. Focus on taking the next step every day.

If you consider everything from a big-picture point of view and don't take any action, you may be overwhelmed and stuck. In the same way, if you focus only on the next action you are taking as part of little steps leading to the larger goal, you may lose sight of why you're going after the goal in the first place. The ideal here is to have a balance of keeping the big picture in mind (remembering what's important to you about the goal and why you're doing it) as you focus on the small steps that actually get you there (taking action each and every day).

Being unstoppably confident means being proactive. Decide what you want and go after it to get it. Sometimes we hear people say "Someday it will happen for me." Or, "I'm just waiting until my ship comes in. I'm waiting for my lucky break. I'm waiting for my big shot." All of the aforementioned sentences are those of reactive people who are waiting to have things happen for them. The problem is that they will be waiting forever. Resourceful people make it happen. Luck is where preparation meets opportunity. Be prepared and relentlessly pursue the opportunities, and you'll surprise yourself at how lucky you become. Go out there and make it happen, because *you are unstoppable*.

Conclusion

This book has presented a number of beliefs, attitudes, and techniques for how to improve your confidence. Some you may love, others you may dislike, others you may have found somewhat intriguing. I salute you for finishing this book because the time you invested in reading this book is an investment in yourself. Few people are up to that task.

Remember that this book only works when you do. These techniques exist to be put into practice. To the extent that you do the drills is the extent to which you will get the confidence skills. Make confidence your habit.

These are techniques I've successfully used to transform my life from that of a shy, antisocial computer nerd into a confident man who speaks in front of groups of people and runs his own business. I know these techniques work because I've done all of them myself. It was a long, hard road for me to break out of my shell and become confident. My major goal in writing this book is to allow you to take a shortcut on your road to unstoppable confidence by learning from my experiences.

Life does not have to be lived in a shell. We don't have to feel anxious around others. We can go after our dreams. The difference between those people who pursue their dreams and those people who stay stuck is the ultimate belief in yourself. That ultimate belief in yourself comes from having confidence, real unstoppable confidence! With your confidence, I know you will take action, never quit, and eventually achieve all of your dreams.

Good luck to you. May all your dreams come true!

qualities to alter your experience and your beliefs

Visual Qualities

Color vs. B/W   [Is the image colored or black and white?]

Size   [How big or small is the image?]

Detail   [How detailed is the image?]

Focus   [How clear is the image?]

Contrast   [Do the elements of the image contrast?]

Brightness   [How bright or dull is the image?]

Border   [Is there a border around the image?]

Distance   [How near or far away is the image to you?]

Shape   [What shape is the image?]

Location   [Where is the image located?]

Perspective   [From what vantage point do you view the image?]

Flat vs. 3-D   [Is the image flat or 3-dimensional?]

Still vs. Movie   [Is the image fixed or is a movie playing?]

Auditory Qualities

Location   [Where is the sound coming from?]

Tonality   [Is it high or low tonality?]

Mono vs. Stereo   [Does the sound surround you?]

Volume   [How loud or quiet is the sound?]

Melody   [Is the sound melodic or monotonous?]
Duration   [Is the sound continuous or intermittent?]

Feeling Qualities

Intensity   [How intense is the feeling?]
Location   [Where do you feel the feeling?]
Speed   [How fast does the feeling occur?]
Duration   [Is the feeling continuous or intermittent?]
Quality   [How would you describe the feeling?]